I Can't Do This!

When Fostering and Adoption Feels Too Hard.

Written by

Fi Newood.

BELONG

Therapeutic Support

Solihull, UK

A Belong Therapeutic Support Book.

First Published in 2018

by Belong Therapeutic Support

in Solihull, Uk

www.belongts.com

British Library Cataloguing In Publication Data

A CIP catalogue record for this book is available from the British Library.

ISBN: 978-0-9926629-4-3

For my wife, Gail.

You sat beside me on those stairs

and have remained beside me ever since.

I love you

(p.s it turns out, we could do it!)

Contents

Prologue

It was 5am on a cold February morning in 2009 and I sat crying alone on the stairs desperately hoping that our 2 foster children had finally gone to sleep.

I couldn't believe that in just six months I had gone from a capable professional with years of experience working in children's homes to this: an exhausted, depressed woman who felt isolated, hopeless and doubted that she had anything left to give.

As I gazed at the bruises and bite marks over my arms and legs I wondered how much longer we could really go on and why nothing seemed to work. We had so much love to give these children but it didn't seem that love was really the magic cure I had previously thought it would be.

Where was all the support they had talked about during our assessment process I wondered angrily? Why had no-one managed to come up with any suggestions that actually worked? Reward charts, time outs, missed activities and other consequences just seemed to be making things worse and I simply could not have yet another conversation with them about how things needed to be better.

Yes, I knew that they had a rough time in their birth family but they were in a loving family now. Surely, they could be so much better behaved. Maybe they didn't want to change. Maybe they were happy trying to get their own way all the time. They didn't seem happy really…. and neither were we.

What would make them happy? Could there be anything else we hadn't tried? What if keeping them here in the chaos and negativity that now defined our lives was stopping them from being somewhere that really could make them happy? Was I doing what was right for them or was I just too afraid that everyone would know I'd failed if we let them go?

And what if we did end their placements? What would that mean for them? Were they destined to bounce from foster home to foster home like so many of the young people I'd worked with before? Or would their next family be their forever home with people more equipped to meet their needs?

What would them leaving mean for us? Sure, we'd stop having to sleep in shifts and wouldn't have all this stress impacting our relationship, but would we ever be able to have a family? Maybe parenting just wasn't for us…. maybe I was just not good at being a mum.

I could no longer think straight. My sleep deprived, stressed out mind was incapable of logical thought at this point and I had come to doubt my own judgement anyway.

So, I simply sat on those stairs and cried and cried and cried until my equally sleep deprived and stressed out wife got up to do the next shift.

"I can't do this" I told her.

"Neither can I" she replied.

And we resolved that something needed to change. We didn't know how but we were going to have to look beyond what we already knew to something different if we were to stand any chance of keeping the boys we had come to love despite everything.

And if that didn't work we'd have no choice but to say goodbye.

Part 1

An Introduction

1. Why I'm Writing This Book.

It was a book that changed everything for my family. It was recommended to me by a therapist I vaguely knew at the time. I ordered it immediately hoping it was the miracle cure for sorting out the mess I felt my family were in.

When it arrived, though, my heart sank. It seemed big, with small writing and a lot of it. A quick flick through showed that it was full of long words that my brain was not able to make sense of and I realised that it was written by a psychotherapist seemly to other professionals.

I discarded it on the bedside table, convinced it wasn't the right book for me.

The truth is, though, that I was scared of reading it. I was convinced that it was going to tell me how it was all my fault; that it was my parenting that was responsible. Surely a better parent would have better behaved kids by now? It had been 6 months since our foster children had come to live with us and things seemed to be getting worse.

What if I read the book and instead of giving me hope it showed me that this situation wasn't going to change? What if it truly spelled out the end of their placement with us?

Two weeks later things were feeling desperate again. I picked the book up and flicked through it. I saw there was a chapter towards the back on parenting so I decided to read that. The first paragraph grabbed my attention, it seemed to sum up our situation perfectly and convinced me to read further, but only that chapter, not the whole book.

The writer did offer me hope and a foundation to build upon. He taught me that what was going on in my family was not unique. It was the unheard stories of many foster and adoptive families. For that I will always be grateful to him.

But still the book was too hard a read overall and not suitable for my very stressed out brain. Whilst it helped me to gain some understanding of what was going on for my children, it did not help me to make sense of my own thoughts, feelings, behaviours and the effects fostering was taking on me physically. Neither did it give me a clear way forward, something that would make this big problem seem easier to tackle.

In the years that have passed I have read many books, spoken with many experienced parents and professionals, attended many training courses and now specialise as a qualified psychotherapist and trainer for foster and adoptive families. It has been a very long process, full of ups and downs along the way and I have learned that so many families have had similar stories filled with similar struggles. We just don't often talk about them. Maybe because we lack safe spaces to do this or maybe because the strength of feeling seems too overwhelming and we fear what may happen if we begin to open up.

Frequently in my work I am transported back to that woman on the stairs and I think what did she need to hear at that time? What did she need to say? What was she able to give brain power to? How did she move from "I can't do this" to "I might be able to do this" to "I am doing this"?

So, I write this book really to her and to all of you parents out there who are having your own version of a crying-on-the-stairs moment.

2. What This Book Is Not About.

This book is not about convincing you to keep your son or daughter or to continue to foster or adopt. I don't know your situation and while I generally believe in keeping families together I also acknowledge that there are occasions when it is best for young people to move on. Ultimately you are the best person to make that decision and I hope that reading this book helps you to make the right choice for everyone involved.

This book is not about telling you that you are a lousy parent either. You're not, and I know that for a fact. How? Because lousy parents do not read books to try and understand themselves and their children better.

We live in a society that promotes the idea of 'perfect parenting'. Such a thing is a myth, it simply does not exist and I have no intention of suggesting it does. If you are a parent you will mess up from time to time. We all do and that's ok.

As none of us get it right all the time, we all have something to learn. This book will encourage you to do that. It will encourage you to learn about your child and about yourself. This may not be easy for you at times, it wasn't for me, but if you can try to be open to this it will pay off. I hope that I will be able to both challenge you and support you in the way in which I write.

3. Why I'm Keeping It Simple.

I know that my readers aren't going to be stupid – fostering and adoption agencies will have already assessed you as being a capable person. But I also know two things:

1. When you feel overwhelmed by parenting you are not able to take in a lot of information.

2. Academics and professionals study therapeutic parenting ideas at great depth and enjoy grappling with difficult concepts. Often, they write in ways that make it hard for parents to understand and make it more complicated than it really needs to be.

This book is designed to be an introduction to the therapeutic parenting ideas that have worked for me. I will be making it as simple as I can while also making it as useful as I can. I cannot cover everything here (it would overwhelm you further if I tried) but I will cover enough to move you forward on your fostering/adoption journey if that is what you wish to do.

At the end of this book I will make suggestions for future learning. I will also discuss how to end a placement as best as possible if that is what is right for your family. To continue parenting a child or to move them on is entirely your decision. Every thought and feeling you have around this is valid. You are not alone in wanting this situation to be better.

I want that for you too. I want to be as supportive as I can for you, so you will find no shaming, judging or unrealistic expectations within this book.

Take your time to read what I write. Take more time to think about how to apply it to your everyday life. It took me many years to feel comfortable in a new parenting style. I feel a long way from that woman on the stairs and yet I acknowledge that she is always with me. I'm forever learning and growing. I hope this book helps you to do the same.

Part 2

The 3B's Therapeutic Model

4. Introducing The 3B's

In my early days of learning about therapeutic parenting I sometimes felt as though the more I heard the more confused I became. This was partly because I was trying to learn new information whilst living in a stressful situation, but also because there were so many different ideas, parenting techniques and advice from professionals that I often felt even more overwhelmed.

Sometimes I could see how different ideas worked together, sometimes I couldn't. Some techniques seemed to make clear sense to me, others felt completely alien to my idea of how to parent.

What I needed was a framework. A clear understanding of how therapeutic parenting works that I could use to help me decide a way forward. Something flexible enough to develop as I learned more, something that could be backed by science, research and practice, something that I could really understand working in practice but was also simple enough for me to go back to basics at times when things were really hard and doing the basics was about all I could manage.

I couldn't find a framework that achieved all of these things clearly enough for me so over the past 8 years I've written one: a therapeutic approach that I have used in fostering, adoption, residential care, education, social work and across my practice as a psychotherapist with great results for both the young people and their supportive adults.

My 3B's model is an attachment-based approach. This means that it focuses on parenting in a way that would create a healthy development for any child but can be used to really understand and work effectively with the difficulties your child may have.

I understand human development to be a result of three things: our biology, our environment and our experiences. Research shows that the most significant factor to influence our development is our experiences of relationships, particularly our first relationship which is usually with a parent.

This chapter will begin by explaining the 3B's model and how it works in an ideal situation – when a child with average needs is born and raised by a parent capable of meeting those needs.

We will then think about what has gone wrong for your child and how it has impacted them.

5. The 3B's in an Ideal Situation.

Through belonging in relationship children develop beliefs about themselves and their world. These beliefs are then visible through the child's behaviour.

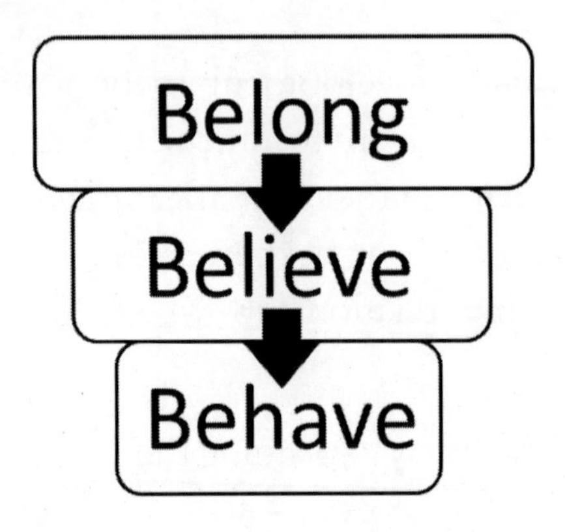

There are two key beliefs that we need to have in order to develop in a healthy way: that we are safe and that we are lovable.

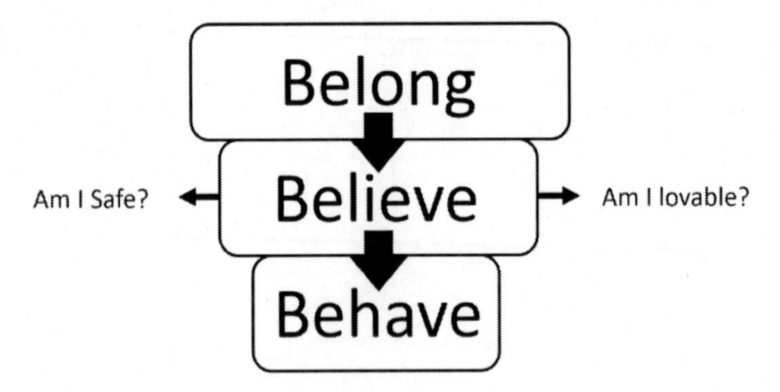

When children believe they are safe they behave in ways that are also safe for themselves and others.

When children believe they are lovable they behave in ways that are loving towards themselves and others.

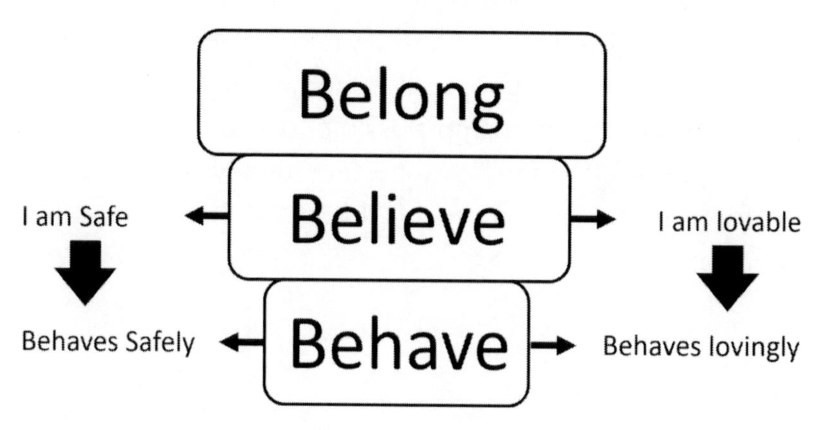

So how do children come to believe that they are safe and lovable? Through relationship.

When parents can keep children safe by setting appropriate boundaries and show them love through appropriate nurture and care the child comes to believe that they are safe and loved enough and behaves accordingly.

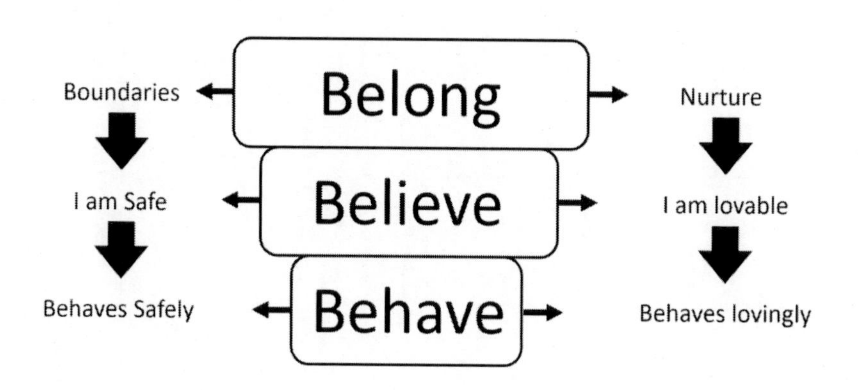

These children then develop into adults who are able to manage their own thoughts, feelings and behaviours.

The 3B's model is the most basic way of understanding how children grow into the people they are capable of being when offered the best relationship possible. Of course, in reality there is no such thing as a perfect family situation and therefore there is no such thing as perfect human development.

6. Understanding How It Can Go Wrong.

Not all children are able to having a boundaried and nurturing relationship with a parent who makes them feel safe and lovable. Some parents are just not available to their children in this way.

Sometimes this is because their needs take priority, sometimes because they are not capable of meeting the needs of their child, and often because they have not experienced enough safety and love themselves to give this to their son or daughter.

For whatever reason (and I make no judgement on these parents) they cannot provide the boundaries and nurture their child needs. Consequently, their child comes to believe that they are not safe enough or lovable enough and this is shown in their behaviour.

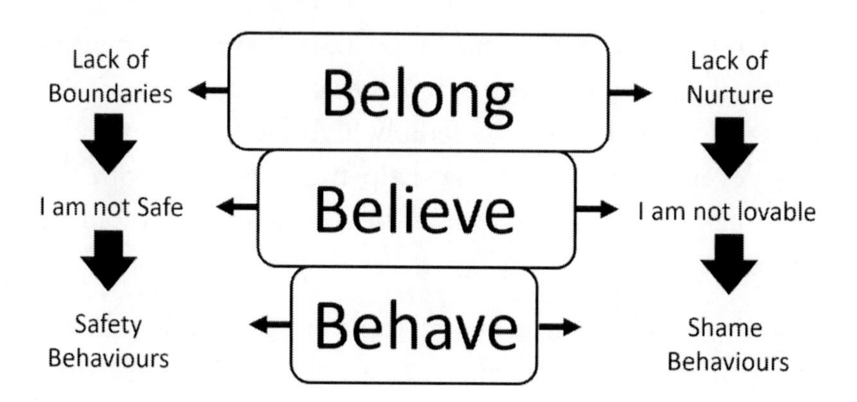

When children believe that the world is not safe their bodies and brain work together to make them behave in a way that feels safer. This is a basic biological survival strategy that the child will often have little control over.

There are different ways this can be seen but essentially it can be understood as the 3 F's: fight, flight and freeze.

Fight: This is where the child fights against what it believes is making them unsafe. For example, a child believes they are going to be hurt by another child and so punches them first.

Flight: This is where the child runs away or hides from a situation that feels scary.

Freeze: This is where a child feels so unsafe that they become frozen, like a stunned rabbit caught in the headlights of a car that doesn't move despite the chances it is going to get run over.

Similarly, when children feel unlovable they develop shame behaviours. Shame is the belief that there is something inherently wrong with you that makes you unlovable. Feeling overwhelming shame is incredibly hard for a person and so they develop behaviours that help them to cope with this. These can essentially be seen as the 3 A's: Attack, Avoid and Appease.

Attack: This is where young people are critical of others as a way of feeling better about themselves or to shift other people's focus away from them to another person in the hope that no-one will see the flaws they believe they have. For example, you ask a child to clean their bedroom, they interpret this request as a criticism of their cleanliness and shout back at you that their brother's room is much worse.

Avoid: This is where children avoid people and situations that make them feel not good enough. For example, a child who believes they are stupid might try to get out of going to school by saying they are ill.

Appease: This is where children try to adapt to what they think other people want them to be in order to become more lovable to them. For example, a boy might feel very emotional but decide not to cry in front of a parent who has expressed that they would see this as a sign of weakness.

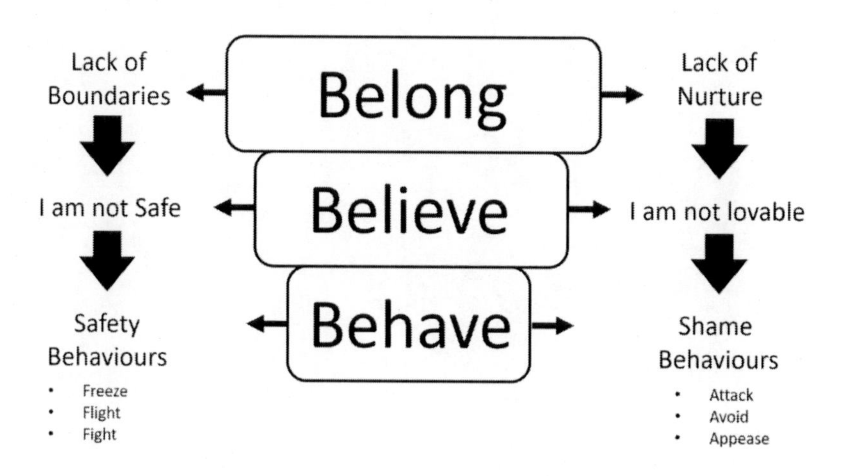

I would encourage you to read this model over until you feel comfortable with it as the 3B's model is the basis for the rest of this book.

This book is now split into 3 sections. The first considers how this 3B's model relates to you and your experiences of fostering/adoption. The second section considers how the model relates to your child and their experiences of belonging, believing and behaving. The third section puts all of this together to consider how you might use this understanding to parent your child in a way that enables you to move forward from where you are now.

Part 3

The 3B's and You

In all the reading I have done around effective fostering and adoption I have never read anything that suggests a model of parenting that makes you, the parent, a priority or that sees your needs as equally valid to your child's.

Sometimes there might be a chapter hidden in the back of a book somewhere that talks about your need to be functioning at your best to do your best for your child. And it is true, but it's not the key message I want to give you.

I want you to know from reading this book that you matter.

You matter just as much as your child does. As much as you want the best for your son or daughter, I want that for you. Not just so that you can be the best for them but so that you can have the best available for you.

If parenting generally has its ups and downs then foster and adoptive parenting of children who've had difficult experiences is like strapping yourself in to the biggest and fastest rollercoaster in the world with no idea of where it is going to take you. Calm for moments, exciting and thrilling at times but downright scary in places too.

At some point you decided for yourself that this was something you wanted to do. It may not have been your first choice to create a family but it was a choice none-the-less. And I don't know anyone who has gone into fostering and adopting and not wanted to make it work for them and their soon-to-be-child.

Maybe you just weren't expecting it to be this hard? I know I wasn't. Despite what I was told, despite my years of working in children's homes, I don't think I really had any idea just how much I was going to be affected personally from caring for my children.

If there is one thing I have learnt over the last 8 years then it's this:

To survive being a foster or adoptive parent, your self-care must be as good as your child-care.

We must consider ourselves as much as we consider our children.

So, the first section of this book is all about you. Because the 3B's model applies as much to you as it does to your child.

7. Belong and You.

This chapter focuses on your relationships with yourself, your child and others. As you read I would like you to consider one question:

'How do I generally deal with relationships?'

Knowing your patterns in relationships, understanding what it is that makes you feel safe and nurtured, and considering your sense of belonging in other relationships (both past and present) may hold clues for ways forward with your son or daughter.

Your Relationship History.

Do you remember all those questions about your previous relationships you were asked during your fostering or adoption assessment? I do.

I remember spending hours with my assessing social worker discussing my relationship with my parents when I was growing up, previous partners, other family members and friends. I felt as though every part of my life was laid bare and at times I couldn't see the relevance. I thought they were asking for a lot of information they really didn't need to know.

I now believe they didn't ask enough.

Whether we like it or not, whether we admit it or we don't, the relationships we had with the people who parented us in our early years have shaped how we view all our other relationships.

If I was to think about all the parents I have been fortunate to meet over the past decade I could clearly designate the majority into 2 different groups:

- People who had good childhoods and want to offer that opportunity to a foster or adoptive child now.
- People who had difficult childhoods and want to help children who are also in difficult situations.

So, let's consider what that might mean for you depending on which group best fits you.

If You Had A Good Childhood.

To grow up in a family that is able to provide you with love and safety is a wonderful thing and an experience that all children should be able to have. The fact that you now want to offer this to another human being is equally wonderful but it's likely that the difference between your experiences of childhood and your child's is going to cause problems. Later in this book I will focus on understanding why this is but for now let's focus on you.

I wonder if you feel frustrated by your parenting experience because you have so much love to give and your child seems so unwilling to receive it. Maybe you feel like you keep on giving to them but it's not making the difference you thought it would. It seems logical that giving love to a child who has not been shown enough of it should work and yet it may not seem this way to you now. I want to reassure you that it does work. Your love will pay out in the end but it is likely to take a really long time if your child has had significant experiences of being unloved in the past. The hardest part is to keep giving love for the length of time this takes.

Another thing to consider is to reflect on your own childhood and try to remember it as it truly was. If there is no such thing as a perfect parent, then there is no such thing as a perfect childhood. There will have been some difficulties for you – there are for everyone. Recognising this can make a big difference in how you understand your relationship with your child.

Equally the way we parent and understand children as a society has changed dramatically over recent decades. Without wishing to enter into debate about the pros and cons of this, I will simply say that what you experienced as good parenting when you were a child may no longer be appropriate today. We can choose to do things differently without it being a reflection on our own parents. After all, your child's needs are probably very different from the needs you had at their age.

Being open to reflecting on the way you parent is so important in fostering and adoption. We all parent the way we were parented unless we make a conscious decision to do it differently. If you aren't sure how to start to do this, here is what I would advise:

Every time you say or do something and think 'I sound just like mum' or 'dad always used to do that' try and tune in to how that feels for you. Does it sit comfortably? How did you experience that as a child? How might your child now experience it?

An example of this for me was the first time I told my son not to answer me back. Gosh, I sounded just like my parents! The memory that came to me was of being a young girl and feeling as though I couldn't express my own opinion, as though I had to agree with the adults because they knew best. I'm sure I am not the only child told this whilst growing up in the 1980's and certainly older generations of my family have strong memories of being told to be 'seen and not heard'. These were clear views of the parent-child relationship that I had unconsciously accepted and was repeating with my children. It didn't sit comfortably and as I reflected I realised that I didn't want this for them. I wanted them to develop their own thoughts and be able to share them. So, since then I have allowed my children to disagree with me, even given them permission to do so – which has led to many conversations about the need to do this respectfully!

If You Had A Difficult Childhood.

Whatever difficulties you had in your childhood I know one thing: you survived them. The fact that you are willing to open your heart up to a child through fostering or adoption is a remarkable thing.

It's also incredibly difficult.

I believe that people who have overcome great obstacles in their own lives can be amazing parents for children with their own difficult experiences. I can see very easily what a child stands to gain from a relationship with someone like you.

The question is, what do you gain?

It is often true that our attempts to heal other people are also an attempt to heal ourselves. By 'rescuing' your child are you really trying to rescue the child that still lives inside you? I didn't realise it at the time, but I was. It's not a bad thing, but it is something to be aware of.

One of the benefits of entering fostering or adoption from this position is that you will have already made some attempts to evaluate the parenting you received and why it was not good enough for you. You will likely have imagined all the ways in which you were going to do things differently and fantasised about how the child might respond to this.

I did. And I was bitterly disappointed when things didn't go how I thought they would.

While I had consciously made a decision to do things differently I was not prepared for how much my unconscious brain was going to keep trying to get me to parent in the same way that I had been parented. Every time I thought about rejecting my children, thought they were not good enough, desired to send them to their bedrooms or considered whether a smack would get them to behave I felt really, really bad about myself. I became really scared of repeating my own parents' mistakes, of parenting in a way that they now regret too.

I can also recognise now that I was being really triggered by my children. Some of the experiences they had had were reminding me of my own and the unloving ways they were acting towards me were not making me feel safe or lovable. I had to learn to separate out what was going on in my present life with what had happened in my past. For me continuing to resolve my previous issues through counselling, learning and personal reflection was the best way to do this.

Your Relationship Template.

Whether generally positive, negative or a mixture of the two, the relationship you had with the person(s) who parented you has created a template for all your relationships.

None more so than the relationship you have with your child now.

You will have entered into parenting your child with a view, largely unconscious, about the way this relationship should go. You will have decided what you need to be like as a good parent and how your child needs to respond.

Many of the difficult feelings you have now are likely to be due to these expectations. You are never going to be the perfect parent and they are never going to be the perfect child. Accepting this is one is of the best ways of moving forward together.

Your Relationship with Your Child.

It is almost certainly fair to say that if you are reading this book then it means your relationship with your child is not what you want it to be. That is perhaps a massive understatement.

In the following section of this book we will be considering your child in more depth and this may shed some light on how they have developed and why they are struggling so much to be in a meaningful relationship with you.

For now, though, let's focus on you.

When we want to become parents we are wanting to connect. No-one wants to parent a child that they do not have a relationship with and yet this may be the situation you find yourself in.

It feels unnatural because in many ways it is. The parent-child relationship is a reciprocal one. The parent may do the majority of the work but they also get their rewards. The hours of hard work teaching your child to walk are seemingly forgotten when you can delight in seeing them take their first steps. You can tolerate the frustration of teaching them to count to 10 when you know that one day you will be struggling to help them with their maths homework. And no matter how many times you deal with their difficult behaviours you know that they love you, that any relationship difficulties can be repaired and that they want a relationship with you as much as you do with them.

But of course, this is generally not the case when you are fostering or have adopted a child with difficult life experiences.

It may be hard for you to delight in your child or to feel any genuine connection. You may find it very hard to love them or even see a time in the future when you could ever have a 'normal' parent-child relationship. It's also likely that you feel bad about feeling this way and ashamed of some of the thoughts you have about them.

And yet I can guarantee that you are not feeling anything that has not also been felt by many foster/adoptive parents: we're just not good at talking openly about it.

It's tiring to give out so much and feel like you get so little back. It does not make you a bad parent, it's completely understandable. We aren't designed to parent in this way.

And yet we can end up taking this all so personally because it feels so personal. I found it hard not to see what was happening between me and my sons as a reflection of who I was. I felt as though they saw the 'real me' and had decided that they didn't want me to be their parent. I felt not good enough and continually rejected. With some perspective now, I can see that this was not the case but at the time it felt so true.

As much as we can behave in ways that trigger unhelpful memories, thoughts and feelings in our children so can our children trigger these in us. I have found it helpful as I have journeyed with this to think about situations with my children and question whether I have ever been in similar situations or had the same kind of thoughts and feelings towards other relationships in my past. Sometimes what I have thought was an issue between me and my child has actually been an issue from my past that I have not dealt with properly. Those feelings of being not good enough and feeling rejected are a good example of this for me.

The other thing that has really helped has been to be realistic about my expectations of our parent-child relationship. My children were too much in survival mode and too distrusting of adults to engage in a loving, reciprocal relationship with me. I had to accept that for a while I may not have much to delight in. I looked for the small things (which had become overlooked) and realised that for my children these small achievements, small moments of connection and hope weren't small at all. They were big and worth noticing.

And ultimately, I realised that if my parenting experience meant putting more in and getting less out than is typical for parents. then I needed to ensure that my needs were met in other ways because they weren't going to be met by my children.

Your Relationship With The 'Hoped-For Child'.

I wanted to briefly recognise here the other reason that many people enter fostering and adoption: childlessness. For many people this is the only viable option to have a family, although it is not often the path that they truly wished to go down.

To be unable to have a biological child is for many people a great sadness. Women (and their partners) may go through years of medical treatments in an attempt to get pregnant and deliver a healthy baby. The pain experienced along the way can be overwhelming and the realisation that this is not something they will ever be able to do can be devastating.

I believe that although these parents may not have chosen fostering or adoption as their first choice for creating a family, they can offer a loving home and family to children who also did not chose fostering or adoption as the way they wanted to be parented.

Many organisations ask that there is a six-month gap after IVF treatment to allow couples to resolve feelings they have about their childlessness. Whilst I understand this, I also feel it is naïve. Issues around childlessness can take a long time to work through and it's likely that these feelings will continue as they become a foster/adoptive parent.

Part of the work is in grieving for the hoped-for child. Whatever way in which we come to fostering and adopting there does come a point whilst parenting troubled young people when it becomes clear that the fantasy of family life that we had built is not likely to be a reality…. at least not anytime soon.

What I see happen then is that parents enter into the grieving process. They begin to mourn the child they wish they had had. They can feel the loss of this 'hoped-for' child just as strongly as a parent whose child has died but they are unlikely to receive the same level of understanding from those around them.

And the difference between the 'hoped-for' child and the child who is living in their house becomes even starker.

It's hard, very, very hard.

In some way there has to become a separation between grieving the loss of one child whilst also embracing the opportunity of another. Because the child you are parenting now may not be your 'hoped-for' child but that does not mean there isn't hope for them and for you.

Your Relationship with Your Birth Children.

Many foster and adoptive parents do of course have their own birth children. The experience you have of parenting your child is very valuable to your parenting role now. It has no doubt taught you a lot and offered you enough of a good parenting experience to want to parent again. But having your own birth children can also be problematic.

Firstly, your concept of the parent-child relationship will likely be stronger than those who have not parented before.

Not only do you know what it is like to be the child in the parent-child relationship but you also know what it is like to be the parent. You know what such a relationship looks like and what does and doesn't work.

At least you think you do.

Whilst there are certainly parenting skills that you have already developed I want you to know that these in themselves are likely to be insufficient when parenting a child who has been traumatised. The rest of this book will hopefully explain to you why these children with additional needs require you to parent with additional skills, but for now I want you to know that whilst you do have a lot to offer, you most likely also have a lot to learn. I say that because many parents feel that they are a failure when parenting their fostered or adopted child. They tend to see all of their parenting as not working and yet so much of it does work and the rest can be learned if the parent is open to do so.

You have been assessed by qualified child-care professionals as being capable of providing good-enough parenting. You are bothering to read this book and willing to learn more. You are not a bad parent. They are not a bad child. It's simply that this child requires something different from what your birth children did.

The other issue faced by many parents is the impact that fostering/adoption has on their birth children. Many parents feel that they chose to foster/adopt and yet their birth children are being affected as a result. This can lead to feelings of guilt and shame for parents and they often end up torn between the different and often conflicting needs of their birth, fostered and adopted children. There isn't the space in this book to do this topic justice but I do think it is worth acknowledging.

Birth children can be hugely affected by their parents bringing more children into the family. Often quite extreme forms of sibling rivalry do play out and birth children frequently resent the way that their parents are treated by the new child and the amount of time and energy their parents have to give to them. However, the effect is not always negative. Many birth children develop significant levels of compassion, love and tolerance when living alongside their new siblings. Their own resilience and ability to understand and deal with life's challenges can also be greatly influenced.

The 3b's model is as appropriate for your birth child as it is for your fostered or adopted child. The overall structure is the same for both, you will just have to apply it differently to meet the different needs of your different children.

Your Relationship with Your Partner.

Some of you reading this book will be parenting without a partner. I truly admire anyone doing so. There are many children who (because of their needs and life stories) benefit from having just one parent to live with. It places a great demand on those parents but is often exactly what those children need.

For the rest of us it is worth discussing the impact that fostering and adoption can have upon our romantic relationships.

The majority of birth parents argue at some point about how to bring up their children. Parenting is tough. It's also a very individual process. We all have different experiences of being parented so it is understandable that we have different ideas of how to parent. Throw in the 'perfect parenting' books, sleepless nights, countless nappy changes and uninvited advice from the mother-in-law and you have the perfect recipe for relationship conflict!

How much more so is this true when you are parenting a child with additional needs – a child that requires so much more but still doesn't come with a helpful manual on how to raise him or her. It is not uncommon for the stress of parenting to play out in your relationship with your partner. You might feel true sadness, disappointment or anger when you think about how your relationship once was to how it is now.

The most common form of relationship dispute that I see in couples is disagreements on how to deal with poor behaviour. One parents wants to be loving and nurturing towards the child and therefore is seen as being too permissive. The other parent thinks boundaries and consequences are the way to go and is seen as being too punitive. This book will address this issue but for now I will say that if as a couple you can offer your child both nurture and boundaries between you then you are half way there already - so keep going.

I want here to focus on what your relationship with your partner has come to mean for you. I wonder if it feels as though this is just one more person to battle with or if you are both on the same page but that page seems to hold no answers and therefore feels hopeless.

I wonder how truly connected you feel to the person you have chosen to spend your life with? They have been assessed as capable of providing love and nurture to a child but are they providing this for you? And in return what are you doing to communicate love back to them? I know that in those early days I was guilty of neglecting my marriage. I became so focused on the children that I forgot there was someone else living in my house who also wanted my love. This was beyond ridiculous given that she was the only person in my house capable of giving me any love back in return!

If we can agree that fostering or adopting has placed huge demands on you as an individual then it stands to reason that it will also place huge demands on your relationship with your partner. What helpful methods do you have in place to deal with this?

What time do you make for nurturing your relationship? How can you discuss the emotional impact of your day-to-day experiences without it becoming an argument if you are both struggling?

What are the boundaries between your roles of parent and partner? How do you ensure that your child does not overwhelm your relationship? That it remains about the two of you instead of being about them?

For us it was important to have a space in our home that was ours alone. The most logical room for this was our bedroom. It became a sanctuary to retreat to and a place that was not caught up in the chaos that came with parenting our children.

We also had weekly date nights. Often these were at home and required little organising but they always followed our date night rule: no discussing the boys. Because making time for one another was not only essential to our relationship but also to meeting our individual needs.

After all, she was the only person in the world who truly knew what was going on in my home and the only person who would tolerate me waking them up in the middle of the night to discuss my latest parenting concern!

Your Relationships with Family and Friends.

18 months after we began fostering we moved to a different fostering agency, meaning that we had to re-do our fostering assessment. It saddened and surprised me to see how many people we had to cross off our previous support network. People who had, prior to the children arriving, agreed to support us in our fostering role but who had since seemed to have vanished from our lives.

The reasons for many of these were obvious. Most of our friends with young children had stopped inviting us over because there was a high chance at that time that one of my kids was going to bite, hit or spit at one of theirs. I could understand that.

Like most parents I now had to juggle socialising with child-care arrangements. There was a limited number of people who I could leave my children with and we had a steady stream of people who offered to babysit, did it once and never offered again! If I was able to find a babysitter or meet up during school hours then often I was either exhausted or too preoccupied with the children to really nurture those friendships. So over time the invites had naturally become less frequent.

When I look back now it is clear to me that at the time of my 'crying on the stairs' moment I was in fact depressed. And like a lot of people with depression I felt so overwhelmed with everything that was going on that even the idea of going out of the house and meeting up with friends exhausted me. So, I had let those relationships just slip away.

Some of our friends and family I was intentionally avoiding. I simply did not want to hear their parenting advice or how 'all children do that'. Where half of them were telling me to be more lenient, the other half were telling me to be stricter. It was too confusing and I felt as though they didn't understand my situation and were judging me. The truth is that they almost certainly didn't understand my situation but were probably trying to help me in the best way they knew how. I wasn't telling them how this made me feel or being clear about what I needed from them and therefore was stopping myself from getting the support I needed. In return they probably felt as though I wasn't appreciating their attempts to help me and might have felt frustration themselves at not being able to 'solve' this problem, so they too began to avoid me.

It wasn't a good situation. One of my biggest learning points since fostering and adopting is that many people do not understand what it means to live alongside a traumatised child but that doesn't mean that they aren't willing to try. What it does mean is that I need to be much clearer about what is going on for me and what I need from them.

One of my other learning points is that not every relationship around me has to become about my children. In fact, it is important for my own well-being that this does not happen. I have now cultivated some great friendships with people with whom I rarely discuss my children or theirs. We actually talk about me and them, about travel, politics, current affairs, last night's TV, anything really, but the point is that they remind me I am more than just a mum. To be a great parent I really need time away from that role to take care of the other parts of myself and to remind myself that I exist and I have value too.

Your Professional Relationships.

If you have adopted your child then depending on where you are in that process will determine whether professional relationships are available to you. In the case of fostering, you will be parenting your child as part of a team of professionals – social workers, link workers, independent reviewing officers etc. The aim of these relationships is to provide support to you and your child but it may not always feel like that.

Each of these professionals will be working to the current legislation around fostering and adoption and will have set ways in which they need to work. The problem this raises for many parents is that legislation is based almost solely on the needs of the child. The experience of the parent is largely overlooked. Despite the frequent instruction legislation, policies and procedures give to provide 'support' for foster and adoptive parents, there is little to suggest what that means in practice or indeed what parents need support for.

Fostering is one of those working roles where it is likely you are being supervised by someone who has never actually done your job. They are almost certainly qualified as a social worker, hopefully have a lot to offer you in terms of their knowledge and experience of working with young people but might not have any idea of how it truly feels to parent a child like yours.

So, your needs may not be so clear to them, particularly if you feel a certain pressure to hide your needs in order to manage that dual (and often conflicting) role of being both a parent and a fostering professional.

I personally feel that we need to develop a greater understanding of what it means to be a professional. Over the time I have been involved in child-related work it has felt as though professional boundaries have become more and more like relationship barriers.

You are not a robot. It is not unprofessional for you to struggle with the great demands of your parenting role. It is unprofessional for your fostering or adoption agency not to recognise this. It is unprofessional for them not to create safe spaces in which parents can discuss the issues they face or provide professional relationships for you that actually do give you the support you need.

Working in a team can bring great benefits but also cause a lot of issues. Maybe you don't like your child's social worker? Maybe your link worker is continually changing? Maybe you feel as though you are desperately trying to do everything you can to make this placement work but those around you are failing to return your phone calls, delaying on making decisions or not taking action when they have agreed to. All of this can be incredibly frustrating. If you already feel as though you are in a battle with your child the last thing you need now is to be fighting with the local authority or your fostering provider.

So, what do you need from the professional relationships around you? Do you need them to listen to you when you are struggling? Do you want them to recommend things that might work? Can they help you find training or learning opportunities? Do you want them to keep you in mind and contact you to see how you are?

Once you are clear what you want and need the next step is making that known to the relevant people. In my experience most professionals would be delighted to have a parent say to them 'actually this is what you can do for me'. They would have been drawn into this kind of work because they want to help people so let them know how they can be their most helpful for you.

Your Relationship with Yourself.

It's strange to think about having a relationship with yourself, and yet we all do. It comprises of the way that we see ourselves, the way that we connect to our own thoughts, emotions, behaviours and bodily sensations and the value we place upon ourselves.

I wonder if in the process of parenting your child you might have lost sight of yourself?

When living with a child with such high needs it can be so easy to neglect our own. We can lose our sense of who we are and shift our focus entirely to the child.

I became so focused on doing everything I could to look after my children that I stopped looking after myself. And yet fostering and then adopting them has offered me great opportunity for self-discovery. I have learned more about myself in my time as a parent than I think I have at any other period in my life. But that had to start with me being open to this self-discovery and for the first few years that was really difficult.

For now, with everything that is going on for you, maybe that's just too much so let's focus on the nature of good relationships and how that applies to your relationship with yourself.

As I showed in my 3B's model, all relationships need both boundaries and nurture. The boundaries help us to feel safe and the nurture helps us to feel lovable. So how boundaried and nurturing are you with yourself?

Do you make space in your diary to look after yourself? Are you clear with other people that this time is important and non-negotiable? Do you do things that help you to get your needs met? Do you even know what your needs are?

How do you nurture yourself? In what ways do you look after your body? Do you have good ways of connecting with your emotions? Are your thought processes helpful or do you get locked in negative ways of thinking? Do you take the time to do the things that make you smile?

For me, the relationship I have with myself is vital to all the other relationships I have in my life. If I do not take time to look after me then I cannot look after anyone else effectively, including my children.

Belonging and You: A Summary

For me, relationships are the meaning of life. How I connect to myself, to other people and to my wider world provides me with my sense of purpose in life, my greatest joy and my fondest memories. Relationships are my source of strength, my comfort in times of difficulty, my challenge to be more of who I am and my reason to keep going.

I believe there is something truly wonderful that happens when two people meet and are able to be completely vulnerable with one another. When everything we are connects with everything they are within the structure of a loving and safe relationship. When we agree to journey alongside one another to the better of us both.

But relationships can also be so bloody hard.

They contain the source of my greatest emotional pain, the memories of unmet needs and the unhelpful patterns that I both knowingly and unknowingly have continued to repeat.

For all the effort I have put into healing the child living in my house, I have had to put more into healing the little child living inside myself. I have had to grow in my ability to be nurturing and boundaried with myself and others. I've had to let go of relationships that weren't helpful to me and learn new ways of being with other people and with myself. None of this has been easy and neither is it a completed task. I am very much a 'work in progress' but I'm okay with that.

Because no matter how many times I have fantasised about being stranded on a desert island with only myself and a good book for company, the reality is that no matter how imperfect my relationships may or may not be, I wouldn't want to be without them.

Questions to ask yourself.

How do I generally deal with relationships?

Is this helpful or are there things I want to change?

What are my expectations of the parent-child relationship and are these appropriate to my son or daughter?

What needs do I have and how are they being met through my relationships?

Do I have needs that aren't being met and what could I do about this?

How can I strengthen my other relationships and build a better support network?

8. Believe and You

In the last chapter we considered your relationships past and present. In this chapter, we will be answering the question 'so what?'. It's easy, perhaps comforting, to think that our past has little bearing on who we are now, that we have moved on and are different people. Yet research increasingly shows that relationships formed in our early years can still be dramatically impacting us decades later, even if those relationships are no longer in our present lives.

That is because relationships shape the people that we are. While some parts of you are likely to be a result of genetics, the majority of what makes you who you are has come from the experiences you have had and how you have adapted to them.

What is of particular importance is the experience you had of early relationships. As a baby you relied almost entirely on your relationship with your parents for your survival. They were the ones tasked with the job of meeting your basic needs and keeping you safe. As you got older and capable of thinking more you came to conclusions about whether or not your parents were safe for you and if they saw you as lovable. This was the starting point of your sense of self-worth.

'Am I safe?' and 'Am I lovable?' are the fundamental questions all human beings seek answers to. Those answers become our core beliefs, we accept them as true even if they are not and live our lives looking for validation of those beliefs.

If you take any unhelpful belief you hold now and work backwards with it I guarantee that feeling unsafe or unloved is at the root. The easiest way to do this is with what I call the 'Why Game'. Officially this has different names (i.e the 'downward arrow technique') but it always reminds me of that wonderfully curious stage that young children go through when all they ever seem to say to you is 'but why?'

Here's a couple of examples taken from previous work I have done with young people.

This was a young person who, despite very difficult experiences, always seemed to be laughing and joking around like nothing bothered him.

YP: I don't cry

Me: Why is that?

YP: Because I'm a boy.

Me: Why does being a boy mean you can't cry?

YP: Because boys don't cry.

Me: I wonder why you think that is?

YP: Because boys are better at being strong.

Me: And what does it mean if a boy cries?

YP: That he's weak.

Me: And what would happen if you were weak?

YP: (laughs) My dad would hit me and say 'stop that nonsense'.

(I wouldn't be safe).

This was a young girl who was an excellent artist but had given up a place at an art college to focus on qualifications that she did not seem keen to do. She was now really struggling with the academic work of her new course.

YP: I have to study hard.

Me: Why is that?

YP: Because I need to get good grades.

Me: What does getting good grades mean for you?

YP: Dunno. That Mum would be happy, I guess.

Me: So what do you think would happen if you didn't get good grades?

YP: She'd be disappointed in me.

Me: I wonder if that might make you would feel like you weren't good enough.

YP: Yes.

(I'm only lovable if I achieve good grades).

When we become curious with ourselves in a gentle and loving way we become more open and able to consider the underlying issues behind our thoughts, feelings, behaviours and bodily responses.

In an ideal situation all children would have relationships that made them feel safe and loved enough to develop good core beliefs but this is not always true and later experiences in life can, and often do, alter a person's perception of their safety and self-esteem.

Let's consider how this might be for you now.

Your Safety Beliefs.

We each will have different ideas about what safety means to us. At its most basic we understand safety as being about survival and the word 'trauma' relates to experience where our lives are put at risk. For instance, a serious car accident would be a traumatic experience for most people.

Are You Actually Safe?

Our starting point when we think about safety is whether or not you are at actual risk of physical harm and to what extent this risk is life threatening.

Some young people, for reasons we will consider later, behave in ways that are very scary to those around them. Despite the fact that they are younger and may be physically smaller they can cause serious physical harm to the people who care for them.

So, my first question is: are you, or someone close to you, at significant risk of harm due to the behaviour of your child? There will be a small minority of people for whom the answer to this question is 'yes'. To those people I want to say this:

Safety has to be the absolute priority. If you or others are not safe then you must take action beyond reading this book. Regardless of whether you have fostered or adopted this child you must get professional support. For children who present this level of risk one or two parents will never be enough, especially if those parents are understandably afraid of their child. You will need a team of people around you and your child.

Your fostering provider or the local authority overseeing your adoption is the best place to find this support. They have a duty of care to you and your child. This is not a situation where I would advise sitting back and waiting to see what support you are offered. You will most likely need to be very proactive in trying to get support in place. You will need to be very clear about what the risks are to any person involved and I would recommend putting this in writing. The organisation or local authority cannot ignore a situation where people may be at significant risk. If you are able to be clear about what support you need, this will also help.

Being Safe vs Feeling Safe.

When you are parenting a child who might actually cause you physical harm, the safety risks are usually easy to see.

But there is a big difference between being safe and feeling safe.

You may know that you are not at risk of death from your child and yet other areas may feel very unsafe for you.

I felt physically and sexually unsafe with my children in the early days because they had no concept of personal boundaries. They would touch me wherever they chose and I was frequently covered in bruises and bite marks. I came to believe that I was not safe around them and this impacted the way I behaved around them and how I viewed the relationship I had with them.

I also felt environmentally and financially unsafe. I can remember being with a friend one night and she was talking about her experience of being burgled. Although the thieves had not taken much they had taken her sense of safety. She was struggling to sleep at nights, didn't like being in the house alone and felt violated by the thought of someone going through her personal belongings.

In that moment I could totally empathise with her but also had strong feelings of anger about the way she was speaking with me. I wanted to shout back that this was what I was dealing with on a daily basis, that I was cross that she couldn't recognise that my children stole from me at every available opportunity and that they routinely went through my personal belongings.

Of course, I wasn't really angry with my friend, I was angry with my situation. And I couldn't really hold her responsible for not understanding how environmentally and financially unsafe I felt because until that conversation I had not really recognised it myself.

I had bought into the belief of the professionals around me that these children steal, they lie and they manipulate to get their needs met. But in accepting this I had denied how I felt about it. I had come to believe that because I had committed to these children knowing all this, I had no right to complain about how their behaviour impacted me. And yet their behaviour was making me feel unsafe and this had changed the ways I behaved around my children and was therefore impacting the relationship I had with them.

Your Safety History.

The number one job of your brain is to make sure that you survive. For that reason, if you have ever been in an unsafe situation (or felt you were unsafe) your brain will have taken note of that experience and remembered it both within your body and also your memory. Your brain will then use these experiences to ensure your safety in the future.

In a lot of cases this works well but sometimes it doesn't. Sometimes your brain can become too easily triggered and think you are at more risk than you actually are.

For example, when I was two years old I was bitten by my cousin's dog. I have no really memory of this event but I was regularly told about it during my childhood. What developed for me was a genuine, and at times overwhelming, fear of dogs. It didn't matter about the size of dog or the breed, it didn't matter if the owner told me how friendly he was or even if he was on a lead. My brain said this dog is an aggressive and unpredictable animal who is going to hurt you.

In a similar way, when I started fostering there were many situations in which I felt out of control and under attack. These situations prompted difficult memories for me of other times in my life where this had also been true. My reactions to what was happening in the present moments with my children became enmeshed with thoughts, feelings, bodily sensations and behaviours that really came from my past. The warning system in my brain was triggered into action more easily than it should have been. I was perceiving the risk as higher than it actually was and my ability to manage the risk as being lower too.

What I learned from this was that the issues in my past had not been fully resolved. I had not developed enough resources within myself to feel safe enough to parent these children. Recognising this alone made a significant difference to me and my relationships with the children. I began to make efforts to separate out what were issues with my children that I needed to deal with now and what were issues from my past that needed to be dealt with at a time that felt right for me. Eventually I had professional counselling during which it became even clearer how much my children had been triggering me.

Later chapters will consider what you can do if you feel unsafe with your child or also recognise that some of what you are experiencing may be related in part or in whole to your previous experiences. For now, though I want to offer some hope. How you are feeling can change. It can improve and feel less overwhelming even if there is no change in the behaviour of your son or daughter. The way that you think and react to your current situation is the one thing that is absolutely in your control. Even if your history of being or feeling unsafe is significant, you can come to a place where this no longer feels as hard as it does now. I see this all the time in parents I work with and I have experienced it for myself.

I no longer react to my children in the same way or to the same extent that I once did. I no longer feel as unsafe with them even now that they are physically teenagers and so much more capable of hurting me than when they were younger.

And I could not imagine my life without dogs.

Your Love Beliefs

When we don't feel lovable we feel shame. Shame is not the same as guilt although a lot of people confuse the two. Guilt means 'I have done a bad thing' whereas shame means 'I am a bad person'.

We all make bad choices from time to time. Guilt is the emotion that allows us to recognise that what we have done is wrong and then look for ways to repair it. Guilt also recognises that it is about what we have done rather than who we are. Someone could do something terribly wrong and hurtful to someone else and still be regarded as a good-enough person. Guilt is not the emotion we are focusing on here.

Shame comes from the belief that you are not lovable, that there is something inherently wrong with who you are that makes other people not accept you.

Shame is also about safety but instead of focusing on physical safety it focuses on our social safety. We are social beings. We survive in this world by being able to connect to other people. Babies are incapable of meeting their own needs. They rely on the people around them to meet these needs for them. From birth they have a number of ways that get people to respond to them. The most obvious of these is crying. Babies are programmed to cry when they need something. Adults are programmed to not be able to ignore a baby's cry. And so, the connection between parent and child begins. As the baby gets older it stops having to wait for the parent to come to them and begins being able to crawl over and initiate that connection themselves.

So, our survival in infancy is entirely reliant upon being able to socially connect. A parent has to be able and willing to connect with us and meet our needs. If they can do this then our sense of self-worth begins to develop. We come to know that our caregiver looks after us because we are valuable to them and this informs the way that we value ourselves.

At its most simple, shame is the emotion of disconnection. It is the fear of becoming isolated from others because of the flaws we perceive we have. It is the sense that our needs can't or haven't been met because we are not valuable enough for those around us to do so.

Your Lovable History.

In an ideal world all children would grow up being showered with unconditional love. They would know that they could be whoever they are and that would always be good-enough. But this is not an ideal world. Most of us grow up with some degree of conditional love experiences. We might feel we were only lovable if we were well-behaved, if we did well at school or if we met the needs of our parents.

No child wants to feel unloved. We will typically go to great lengths to gain and keep our parents' attention and appreciation. We will adapt parts of ourselves to meet what we believe are the expectations of our parents. For me this meant taking the role of caregiver at a time in my life I should have been a care-receiver. As the eldest child, I learned to get recognised by looking after other people and having pseudo-maturity. This made me lovable, recognised and appreciated by my parents. It is therefore not a great surprise that I have as an adult made a career out of helping other people.

I wonder what your experiences of love have been so far in your lifetime. Did you grow up knowing that you were loved and cared for by people who could show you that? Did you adapt parts of yourself to meet the needs of other people? If so, are these adaptations helpful to you today?

Being Lovable vs Feeling Loved.

There is a world of difference between being loved and feeling lovable. I believe that all people regardless of who they are or what they have done in their lives are worthy of love.

Most people can accept that there are parts of themselves that are loved by other people. But it is hard for a lot of people to see the whole of themselves as worthy of love. We tend to set very high and unrealistic expectations upon ourselves about the kind of people we feel we should be. The parts of us that don't live up to these expectations we then try to hide from other people and often from ourselves.

This is particularly true when it comes to the parenting part of ourselves. Our society is flooded with messages about parenting that suggest that only perfect is ever really good-enough.

And yet rationally most people know that the 'perfect person', and therefore the 'perfect parent' is a myth. That it is part of being human to make mistakes and to be imperfect. We can often show great love and acceptance to other people about the very same qualities that we struggle to love and accept within ourselves.

Being able to feel good-enough as a person is hard for most people. It is exceptionally hard for parents who are caring for traumatised children – children who almost certainly do not feel good about themselves or believe that their new parent will be able to be a good-enough parent for them.

I wonder if this is the position you find yourself in with your child. Maybe they continually tell you how rubbish they think you are. Maybe they reject you as being not good-enough not only as a parent but also as a human being. Maybe they know things about you that make you feel vulnerable and ashamed and therefore make you feel emotionally unsafe with them.

Maybe you simply wonder if you can ever be a good-enough parent for them to ever love you back.

Believe and You: A Summary

Our beliefs about being safe and lovable often become entwined. Where one is about physical safety, the other is about emotional safety. Both beliefs centre on our need for survival as the next chapter will show and both beliefs are born out of our relationships with others as our last chapter did show.

Are you safe enough and loving enough as a parent was the key questions answered by your fostering or adoption assessment. Not only have you been approved as both safe and loving by the social worker who made that very detailed report but it has also been agreed by a panel of people who were considered knowledgeable within the fostering or adoption context.

You are good-enough as a person and as a parent.

Questions to Ask Yourself.

Am I safe?

Do I feel safe?

Do I need to do anything about this?

Am I lovable?

What parts of myself do I feel good about?

What parts of myself do I not feel good about?

Am I open to learning more about myself by reading the next chapter?

9. Behave and You

As our last two chapters have shown, the relationships and life experiences you have had have created beliefs for you about how safe and how lovable you are.

This chapter will show how this influences the way that you behave.

A lot of parents come to me with great shame over the behaviours they engage in. They report the times of losing their temper, the desire to reject or hurt their child, their attempts to run away from the situation or how they perceive they are 'taking it out' on other loved ones around them.

I have no desire to increase the shame you might feel about the ways you are behaving. I do not believe you are a bad parent. What I would like to do is explain why you are behaving in the way you may be. I believe that understanding ourselves is often the first step to changing those parts of ourselves that we feel uncomfortable with and which might be causing ourselves or others difficulties.

Just as all our thoughts and feelings relate to our beliefs about being safe and lovable so do our behaviours and bodily reactions.

Safety Behaviours.

If the last chapter highlighted to you that you hold beliefs that you are unsafe either due to your relationship with your child or due to previous experiences then it might be really helpful for you to understand what happens in your brain when these feelings of unsafety are triggered.

Our brains are really quite incredible. They are also highly complex. I am aware that many parents reading this will be living in very stressful situations so I want to explain how your brain functions in a very simple way.

This is the Brain Switches metaphor that I use with all of the children and stressed out parents that I work with.

I want you to imagine that your brain is made up of millions and millions of switches. For everything you do there is a switch. There's a switch for breathing, a switch for getting dressed, a switch for laughing, a switch for talking etc.

These switches make up three parts to your brain.

The survival part of your brain is made up of your most basic switches. They are there to keep you alive. Switches that help you to breathe, sleep, eat, and keep you safe from danger.

The emotional part of your brain is made up of switches that allow you to feel connected. Switches that help you to feel emotions, connect to other people and remember key experiences.

The thinking part of your brain is made up of switches that allow you to think. Switches that help you to be rational, to evaluate, to understand situations and to communicate effectively.

For a lot of the time these different parts of our brain function really well together but this changes in times when we think or feel very unsafe. In these moments our brains go into pure survival mode. Almost all brain activity comes from the survival part of our brain. The thinking part of the brain shuts down almost completely and, depending on the degree of threat, the emotional part of our brain might do this too. Have you ever been in an experience that has been so stressful that you 'can't even think straight'? I think most of us probably have and it's a great example of how in times of stress we cannot access our thinking brains.

When the survival part of our brain feels unsafe it has a number of different switches it can turn on. The biggest of these are the freeze, flight and fight switches. Your brain will probably have a preference for which one to turn on for you. It is likely to be the one that you have used the most during your life time. It will turn on that switch and keep it on until it believes you are safe enough.

So, let's consider now how feeling unsafe might turn on those survival switches and what this could mean for your behaviour.

The Freeze Switch.

The freeze switch is typically the first switch to be turned on by the survival brain. This is that moment when you are aware of your situation but don't know how you are going to handle it.

A couple of years ago I was involved in a car accident on the motorway. Another car hit the driver side of my vehicle and as soon as I became aware of that impact I froze. I could see that I was going to hit another car but, in that moment, I couldn't do anything to stop it. It all happened very fast. I did go into the back of the car in front and then sat in my car for a few moments unable to really comprehend what had just happened – not helped by the man in front shouting at me! Thankfully no-one was hurt and my freeze switch turned off pretty quickly to allow me to deal with the fact that we were cutting off two lanes of motorway traffic and other cars didn't seem keen to slow down.

In other situations, people typically move from the freeze position and then into fight or flight. The freeze switch is designed not to be on for too long because it does in fact make you vulnerable. If you are about to be attacked your body does need to assess the situation quickly and then move to either fight off the attacker or run away from her.

However, there are certain situations in which people experience a prolonged period of time in which they are in freeze mode. Typically, this happens when there is not the option to fight or to flight. Many people who are sexually attacked find themselves in this position. Unable to escape or fight their attacker they remain frozen. Often, they report feeling numb at the time, being aware of everything that is happening but it is as though it is happening to someone else and not them.

In therapy they raise feelings of overwhelming shame. They believe that in not fighting back they allowed their attacker to do what he or she did. This is not true. They had absolutely no choice in the matter. In actual fact it is a sign that they have a very well-functioning brain. Imagine if in that moment of being attacked they had been fully present. The thoughts, feelings, behaviours and bodily reactions they would have experienced would have been totally overwhelming. So, unable to actually move away from this unsafe situation the freeze switch has allowed them to, in some way, escape within their head until the situation is over and they are safe enough to think and feel again.

The Flight Switch.

When the flight switch is turned on in the brain it causes us to want to escape the situations we are in. When under extreme attack we might run as fast as we can to get away. This is because your brain is trying to ensure your safety. It will make your body as prepared as possible to run as fast and as far as you can to escape the danger.

In a less extreme situation you might find yourself backing away from your child or leaving the room entirely. It is not uncommon for foster and adoptive parents to go to another room and lock themselves away from their child until they feel safe enough to be around them.

The Fight Switch.

Another switch that gets turned on by the survival brain is the fight switch. As its name suggests, this is the switch that makes you want to fight physically in times when you feel unsafe.

If your brain sees your child as a significant threat then you might lash out physically towards them. More commonly I see parents use their bodies in a way that matches the level of physical threat they perceive from their children. They might stand in doorways to show that they control whether or not the child leaves the room, they might square up to the child making their body taller and wider, they might shout or make threats of harm.

Clearly this is not helpful but it is very understandable from a biological perspective.

I wonder if in reading this you can identify the switch that gets used most for you? When you feel most afraid do you want to run or do you fight it out? Could that help explain behaviours you might currently be displaying?

Shame Behaviours.

Shame behaviours work in a very similar way. When we feel unlovable our brain sees this as a social threat and has a need to protect itself from potential harm. It has a number of switches available to do this and the thinking part of the brain tends to not be very involved in the decision-making here either.

The main shame-based switches are attack, avoid and appease. All of them are aimed at preventing people from focusing on the parts of ourselves that we feel are unacceptable. So, let's consider them now.

The Attack Switch.

Have you ever in the middle of an argument found yourself shouting something at the other person that you know is really hurtful to them. You most probably didn't even really believe what came out of your mouth and if you had been thinking more you probably would never have said it. But you did and now it is out there and you know you can't un-say it.

This would be using your attack switch and I don't think there is anyone who at some point in their lives hasn't done so. I can almost certainly guarantee though that if you played that argument back you would see that prior to your attack switch coming on something had happened that had made you feel unlovable.

One of the easiest ways to protect ourselves from criticism is to criticise other people. We do not attack only in arguments we can do this in smaller and less obvious ways too. People who do not feel good about themselves often say and do things to make other people not feel good about themselves either. It is a behaviour that many of us recognise as 'playground bullying' and yet it is something that we are all capable of doing to different extents in different situations.

When we use our attack switch we hope to create a diversion. We want to move people's attention away from the parts of ourselves that we don't want them to focus on and onto something or someone else.

What we also do in this is question the authority of the person who has made the observation of us that we are uncomfortable with. What we are in effect saying is 'how can you criticise me when you are so flawed yourself'.

It is a very clever way of defending ourselves. All people have parts of themselves that they feel ashamed of and attacking those parts in another person does usually divert attention away from us in the moment. It can of course be incredibly hurtful.

Whoever stated that 'words can't hurt' was clearly in denial. Words can and do hurt. They can attack us to our core, change how we see ourselves and create an impact that is debilitating.

When I worked in children's homes I had a choice about how well I allowed the children I cared for to get to know me. I have that same choice now as a therapist. I have very little choice though when it comes to the people I live with. My children know me really well. Therefore, they know exactly what to say to hurt me. I also know them and know exactly what to say to hurt them. We are capable of attacking one another in a very meaningful way and in the past, this has happened on both sides.

When our attack switches go off there is always repair needed to the relationship.

The Avoid Switch.

The avoid switch is often a subtler way of defending ourselves from feelings of being unlovable. We simply avoid the people and situations in which those parts of ourselves that we don't like might be exposed.

For example, I have a love-hate relationship with public speaking. Much of my career has required it, when I'm doing it I tend to enjoy it and the feedback I get after speaking or delivering training is always very positive – suggesting it is one of the things that I am good at.

There is however a part of me that dreads it because of experiences in my childhood. As a child I often felt a lot older than many of my peers. Various experiences meant that I had matured quickly and therefore so had my interests and level of conversation. This meant I often felt very different and when communicating with people of my own age I struggled to explain myself well or to feel that they understood what I was saying.

In my late teens I was diagnosed with the condition of aphasia. It affects language processing and means that I would often get words muddled up – say one word when I mean another. Although this has significantly improved for me over time and I have learned various ways of managing it, I am still haunted by the memory of being thirteen and standing in front of my science class to deliver a speech on living organisms - if only that was the word I had used!

Earlier this week I was asked to speak on radio for the first time about working therapeutically with teenagers. My initial thought was to say I was busy that day (I wasn't) or to not contact the radio manager back. This would be my avoid switch wanting to protect me from what it thought might be another humiliating experience that made me feel not good enough.

Understanding this meant I said "yes".

The Appease Switch.

There are times when we are faced with a choice about whether or not to be our true selves. Sometimes, we decide to flip our appease switch instead to make ourselves more appealing and therefore more lovable to other people.

Have you ever been in a social situation with people you don't know very well and a topic comes up in conversation that you have strong views about. I wonder how you respond. Where some people might be very confident in sharing their views, many people are not. They will hold back and wait to see what other people say before deciding whether or not to give their opinion. They might even find themselves saying they believe something when, really they do not.

This is one example of how we might appease. Instead of being true to ourselves we go along with everyone else, we act like the person other people expect us to be in order to be more likable to them.

I knew at the time of putting it on that my pink, green, purple and white 1980's shell suit was hideous but I still wore it. Why? Well because everyone else had one. My teens were spent listening to whatever horrendous song the latest boy band had released, not because I liked the music but because my friends did. And I did not particularly want to hang around in a park on a cold Friday night drinking cheap cider from a bottle but apparently this was the cool thing to do.

We can see the appease switch working hard throughout our adolescence. It's a time in which we try to work out who we are and what that means. Peer pressure to fit in is high and we can easily be conditioned to behave according to how the world around us (especially our friends) tells us to be.

For a lot of people this continues way beyond teenage years. The desire to be accepted means that so often we go along with being what we think other people want us to be. But how many of us ever really manage to 'keep up with the Joneses and is Mr or Mrs Jones really the person we want to be anyway? Are they even happy themselves?

If we do use our appease switch to become more acceptable to other people then how can we ever genuinely feel accepted when we still are hiding parts of ourselves.

We truth is we can't. Often the defences we put in place to protect ourselves from social shame increase our own private sense of shame instead and we worry about getting found out.

Behave and You: A Summary

So, what does all this mean?

Well, it means that we need to stop seeing a person's behaviour in isolation. We have to understand that all behaviour is really just how we show the outside world what is going on in our inside world.

Under extreme stress we will have little control over how we behave. We will simply communicate through our actions the safety and shame beliefs we hold because of the relationships and experiences from our past and our present.

In understanding this we can begin to stop feeling ashamed of the things we do or blaming others for the things they do and start to look at ways of changing the underlying causes. This is really the only way we can change our behaviour in a meaningful and lasting way.

So, instead of looking at your safety- and shame-based behaviour and feeling bad, I would encourage you to learn from it.

Questions to Ask

What does your behaviour tell you about how safe and loved you feel right now? What does it show you about the relationships around you?

What does it show you about your relationship with yourself?

10. The 3B's & You: A Conclusion.

This first part of the book has focused on you, the parent. If you have made it this far without giving in to the temptation to flick over to the chapter on your child then well done. It is all too easy to focus our attention on our children. In doing this we suggest that they are the only ones with difficulties and the answers to our current situation rest solely with them. This is not true. Being willing to examine yourself will be a crucial part to your success as a foster or adoptive parent.

In this first part of the book we have examined how you might understand your own sense of belonging, beliefs about safety and love and the behaviours you might be displaying. In the next part we will examine the same for your child.

In the third section we will bring all of this together to look at how you can improve your relationship with your child and how you both can move towards feeling safer and more lovable. We will also look at how to work with behavioural issues whilst this is happening.

Part 4

Belong, Believe, Behave and Your Child

In the last section we were thinking about how the 3B's model fits for you as a parent. Hopefully it gave you some insight into how belonging, believing and behaving work as individual themes and also how they relate to one another.

As a parent I think I am incapable of reading anything and not thinking about how it relates to my child. I wonder if you are the same? As you have gone through the first section of this book, have you already started to make some sense of how the 3B's might also relate to your child?

Everything I have written so far is generally applicable to your child. There is a reason for this. We often talk about fostered and adopted young people as though they are completely different from anyone else and yet the reality is that they aren't. We have more in common with the children in our care then we might be comfortable to admit.

Just as my children can feel unsafe, so can I. Where they can be triggered into the safety behaviours of freeze, fight and flight, I can too. And I'm willing to admit that the times I feel unlovable can also leave me equally capable of attacking, avoiding and appeasing.

I think often the best way to understand our children is first to have a true understanding of ourselves. Instead of continually focusing on their difference from us and others, it can be helpful to start by considering how we are the same. That is why I made the section that focused on us as parents the first section of this book.

Somehow it also helps me to know that these creatures living in my home are not aliens from a different planet. They are simply three young souls who have had life experiences that have caused them to develop as they have. And the reality is that any of us, given the same situation, would likely have developed in the same or similar ways.

Many foster and adoptive parents have not had a personal experience of childhood trauma. Some parents have, but maybe not in the same way or to the same extent as the child living in their care. That's ok but can lead to a lack of understanding of the child, the impact their life experiences have had upon them and how best to parent them now.

This next section of the book will consider further how abuse, neglect and other forms of trauma may impact your child's ability to belong, believe they are safe and lovable and behave accordingly. Some of what I write may also be appropriate to you depending on your history. I would encourage you to reflect on yourself when reading about your child, in the same way that you (no doubt) reflected on the child when reading about yourself.

11. Belong and Your Child.

As I have already shown, relationships are incredibly important to our development. Although we are also impacted by our biology and other life experiences, research is showing that the first relationship we have with a caregiver is highly significant.

In the 1930's three of my uncles were placed in care. It was an act of love and desperation by my great-grandfather. His wife had suddenly died and he was unable financially, practically, or emotionally, to care for four young children. My Nana was the eldest, aged just 9yrs. She remained living with her father and it was several years before the family was stable enough for the boys to return to live with them.

In that era, theirs was not an uncommon story. Also common was the number of unmarried women whose children were placed for adoption to avoid the shame associated with pre-marital sex at that time. These were very sad situations but they are not typical of the experiences of fostered and adopted young people today. Most of our children have experienced abuse, neglect or other forms of trauma. I don't know your child's history but, based on the fact that you are reading this book, I can be certain that they have had relationship experiences that have left them feeling unsafe and/or unlovable.

I'm aware that as I wonder what your child has experienced, you might be wondering that too. I believe strongly that foster and adoptive parents should know all of the information around a child placed in their family. However, this wasn't my experience and it doesn't appear to be the experience of many. There are lots of reasons why this might be the case, but in honesty I've yet to hear one that makes sense if we are wishing to give children the best possible chance to succeed.

As we build relationships with our children their histories do start to become clearer. The more safe and lovable a child feels, the more likely they are to reveal aspects of their past life. The more situations we expose them to, the more we can learn from being curious about their reactions. It was my son's meltdown over being given a toy fire engine that revealed to me a trauma experience he had surrounding fire. It gave me specific questions to ask his social worker so I could gain the information that was necessary for me to parent him best.

Relationship Glasses.

There is an activity I recommend to parents, have done with my own children and also with those I work with. It's one of those pieces of work that is always enlightening. Providing I've built a generally good relationship with the child and I've caught them at a good time, this activity offers me great insight into their experiences and offers the child a great way to understand their current relationships.

I start with a drawing of a pair of glasses. I explain that when babies are born they look at the world and their parents through clear lenses. Everything for them is a new experience. Sometimes that is exciting but sometimes it's scary. I ask the child to imagine what it would be like for them if everything they did always felt completely new to them. I ask them about any upcoming events that they might be looking forward to and why this might be. How do they know that going to the park or a party is something to be happy about?

This moves us into a discussion about predictability. I explain that every experience we have creates a memory. We then use our memories of the past to help us make sense of our present and prepare for the future. This makes the world feel more predictable and therefore less scary. I explain that the most important experience for a baby is the experience of being in a relationship with his or her parents.

We then create an imagined child together. A child who has had excellent parenting. We begin to imagine about what experiences this child might have had and what they might have learned from those relationships.

Across one lens of the glasses we will write what that child has learned about parents. For example:

- Mums are loving.
- Dads give great cuddles.
- Parents give you nice food.
- Dads look after you when you are poorly.

Across the other lens we write about what this means for the child. For example:

- I am lovable.
- I am safe
- I can trust my parents
- People are kind.

We then move on to a second pair of glasses and a second imagined child. I tell them that this child has not had good-enough parenting and together we create a story around what this might mean. Generally, I let the young person lead this part and so far, I have found that every time they have created a character who has had very similar experiences to their own. There is a reason for this. Children (like all of us) will typically draw on their own life experiences when asked to be creative. Many of our young people have not reached the developmental stage that allows them to fully use their imagination and so their character will be based a lot on what has happened to them.

For a child to talk about their actual life story can be highly shaming. They also can have a variety of feelings about speaking negatively about their birth parents. However, if I ensure that I talk about the created character rather than the actual child, I find that children really open up. They often reveal information that was previously unknown.

When I ask the question, 'What has this child learned about parents?' I receive answers such as:

- They are mean.
- Sometimes they don't give you food all day.

- They get really angry when they smell funny (have drunk alcohol).
- They make you do all the cleaning.

When I ask the question, 'What does this mean for the child?' I receive these kind of answers:

- She doesn't think anyone will ever like her.
- He has to steal food.
- He tries to be a good boy so nothing bad will happen
- She doesn't want a new mummy because mummies are mean.

In a very non-direct way the child is often telling me their story. It is how they see being in a parent-child relationship. We then talk about how the different pairs of glasses look now that they have been written all over. Some young people chose to colour them in. If they do, the first pair of glasses are always coloured in beautifully and with bright, attractive colours. The other pair tends to be scribbled over in dark colours.

We talk about how the experiences we have in those early years create a relationship template – or in this case, a relationship pair of glasses. I tell them that not only would this child wear the glasses when looking at their parents but they would actually be wearing the glasses when looking at every person they meet.

Then we do some wondering. I wonder what it would be like if you had to wear one of these pairs of glasses all the time? I wonder what these glasses might make you think about a new teacher? I wonder which one you would most like to wear? If you were wearing the nice glasses and someone bumped into you, what might you think? I wonder if this would be different if you had the other pair of glasses on?

There are so many questions you can ask to explore these ideas with them. This activity typically takes several sessions and is something I continually come back to. It really is a good activity to help a child make sense of their history and how it impacts their present life. It also allows us to say things to the created characters that we wish to say to the actual child. For us parents, it can be rich with information about our children's relationship experiences.

How your Child Sees You

When your child looks at you, they aren't looking through clear lenses. They are looking at you though the lenses created by their birth parents and any other previous parenting figures. Whatever experiences they have had with them, they will expect to have with you. In short, your child expects you to abuse or neglect them.

I've been a foster-adopt parent now for ten years. I've spent around nine and a half of those years being told that my children should be 'ok' by now. Family, friends and professionals alike have said that if we provide a loving family home then our children will soon settle. That is not my experience. It is not the experience of the many, many parents I know who are also fostering or adopting. The relationship template that traumatised children have is strong. For reasons I will explain soon, it will not go away quickly or easily. It took 3-5 years for my children to have any genuine trust in me as a parent. They often still do not truly see me as I am and will revert back to mistrust very easily.

That is one of the hardest parts of my parenting experience. The relationship I have with my children is so heavily influenced by the relationship they had with their birth parents. I often have felt as though I am taking the consequences of someone else's actions. Although I try really hard to be compassionate towards their birth parents, I have also had feelings of anger, resentment and injustice because of the impact their parenting has now had on me too.

One thing that has really helped me is to create a distinction between how my children see me as a parent and who I really am. I understand that when they attack me, they are attacking the idea of a parent. When they steal, they steal from the parent template. They can both love me and also hate the parent that I represent. It's an important distinction that helps me not to take too much of my children's behaviour to heart. I just have to remember to think that way in the moment, which is not always easy.

How Your Child Sees Themselves.

The relationship template is not just about how the child sees their parent figure, but also how they see themselves.

If you remember back to earlier in this book, I told you that how we are treated by our parents is one of the very early stages of developing our self-worth. When children are treated in loving and safe ways they come to believe that they are worthy of this treatment. Sadly, this works in the opposite way when children are treated poorly.

I have never worked or lived with a traumatised child who has not believed that they were responsible for the abuse they experienced. I have worked with young people with the most horrendous life stories – children passed around paedophile rings, raped in infancy, locked in rooms for days at a time, those whose survival alone is astonishing – in every case, they have blamed themselves.

They say that the only truly unconditional love is the love a child has for their parent. It is desperately sad to see a young person have so much self-hatred for something that is absolutely none of their responsibility.

The one relationship that goes everywhere with us, is the one we have with ourselves. Children who feel not good-enough experience this continually throughout their daily life. If these feelings are not worked with, then they will remain with them for the rest of their lives. They may become good at hiding the depth of these feelings from others but they will not be able to hide it from themselves.

The relationships they create with themselves will often mirror the relationship they had with their parents. Instead of keeping themselves safe they will often have poor skills around boundary setting, structuring their time and knowing when and when not to take risks. Instead of nurturing and loving themselves, they will often have a very negative inner voice, behave in ways that increase their sense of shame and be very self-punishing.

Even very young children appear to have clear ideas of who they need to be in order to gain approval or simply survive their world. Whatever ways they learned to be in relationship with their birth families, will be the same ways they will try to be in relationship with you. They don't know any different.

Belong and Your Child: A Summary

Being in relationship is something we learn. We first learn how to be with our parents and then apply this learning to all the other people who come into our world. Through parent interaction we learn how to form other relationships and maintain them by developing our social skills. A good-enough parent-child relationship will usually lead to a child developing other good-enough relationships.

Foster and adoptive parents often experience something different. Our children can find it easier to make relationships outside of the home, especially with adults. It can be really hard to see your child getting on better with one of your relatives then they do with you. This can also lead to an even poorer understanding from that relative (and others) about what is really happening in your home.

A lot of parent shaming can happen on these occasions. The notion is that your child doesn't get on with you because of who you are and the approach you are taking to parenting them. It's usually not true.

The reality is that this other adult is not the child's parent. They don't have to engage with the child in a parenting capacity. Therefore, the parenting template that the child has does not largely apply. If this relative was to suddenly have to parent the child - because you've reached the end and turned up with them and all their belongings on the relative's doorstep! – they would soon be having all of the same difficulties that you are currently having.

My children and I would have got on really well from the start if I didn't also have to be their mum. In fact, this was our experience with our youngest child. We developed a relationship with him over an 8-month period through his brother's contact sessions, not knowing that he would one day become our son. The child I experienced whilst providing contact engaged with me very differently when I later came to parent him.

The other thing that I think is really worth mentioning is the difference between genuine relationship and the appearance of relationship. Many fostered and adopted young people have a lot of relationships around them and yet when examined closely you realise that they are not always genuine.

Some relationships are very superficial, they appear close but actually aren't. Some relationships are fleeting as the child lacks the ability to sustain them. Many relationships are unhealthy for one or both parties.

Just as with children who have a good-enough parenting experience, your child will likely have to get their relationship with you right before being able to form genuine loving and safe relationships with anyone else.

Questions to Ask

How might my child have got his or her needs met in the birth family?

How have they managed to survive so far?

Were their parents willing and able to meet their needs at least some of the time or did the child get very good at meeting his or her own needs?

What needs weren't met and how did they deal with this?

12. Believe and Your Child.

The experience we have of early relationships create memories. We use these memories to help us make sense of the world around us. If we have generally good memories then we will come to believe that we are both safe enough and lovable enough.

Your Child's Memory of Early Experiences.

Some of our children will have been very young when removed from their birth families. Many people will tell you that they are too young to remember what they experienced. I wish that were true but sadly it is not. Babies and very young children do remember their experiences of birth families but not necessarily in a cognitive way.

The part of our brain which holds emotional and bodily memories is called the Amygdala. It matures in the womb, meaning that even before we are born we remember our emotional and bodily experiences. The part of our brain that stores thinking memories (the stories of what happened to us, the order of those experiences etc) is the hippocampus, which informs the thinking brain. This typically begins to develop around the age of 3yrs.

If your child experienced difficulties in the first few years of their life, they will have an emotional and bodily memory but won't have the thinking memory to make sense of it. So, they might find loud noises really, really scary but not understand that this is because they were often shouted at for long periods of time. They might have uncomfortable sensations in their bodies but not understand that this is normal hunger that feels intolerable to them because their bodies were often left without food when they were a baby.

If your child experienced difficult situations after the age of three they might have thinking memories of what happened. Some might be able to tell you the story of the event but many won't be able to do this or will only remember fragments.

It is very common for people of all ages to have very difficult experiences and lack a full memory of what happened. If we return to think about the three brains you will remember that when we are in a scary situation we go into survival mode. This means that the main part of brain that is functioning is the survival brain. There is some function in the emotional brain but very little in the thinking brain. With our thinking brain largely switched off, we may not have a clear thinking memory. We may be like a very young child with only emotional and bodily memories of what happened.

So, we have to understand then that the beliefs your child has developed about their physical and social safety are not all thought based. A lot of the beliefs are held in bodily and emotional experiences.

The Power of a Belief System.

Our belief systems are very powerful. They have to be to keep us safe. It's important that we use our experiences to predict whether or not we are at risk. If a child has learned that parents are a risk to the physical or social safety then they will not let go of that belief easily. Many foster and adoptive parents (myself included) get frustrated when their child won't trust them. That's completely understandable from the parent perspective.

But if we think from the perspective of the child then we have to say, why would they trust us? In fact, why would they ever trust anyone? Some of our children have been so badly hurt in the past that to trust us now would be to take a huge risk. It would mean making themselves very vulnerable and they know more than most what the consequences of vulnerability can be.

Our children are never going to see us through clear lenses. They can't erase the experiences they have had. The best we can hope is that they have enough good experiences with us to counteract the impact of the bad experiences they've had before.

Changing a child's relationship template is not easy. They will hold on to it until they either feel safe enough with you to let it go or willing to take a massive risk. And that can take a really long time. A major factor in this process is belief bias.

Our beliefs create the glasses that we see the world through. We need the world to be predictable in order to feel safe. Therefore, we need to believe that our glasses are accurate. So, we look at the world through those glasses and seek confirmation that the glasses are correct. If a child has a belief that adults are mean, they will look for evidence to prove that this is correct. If a child believes that they are unlovable they will largely ignore anything that suggests otherwise. In doing this the child strengths the beliefs they hold.

To complicate matters further, many of our young people engage in a thinking behaviour called splitting. This is where they see everything as either completely good or completely bad. Sometimes this is referred to as 'black and white' or 'all or nothing' thinking.

This is a real problem for me. I don't know about you, but I am not a perfect parent. Far from it. I screw up. I say things I shouldn't. I forget about their school bake sales and I'm no way near as cool as their friend's mum. Whilst this might be tolerable to another child, it's often not tolerable to mine. My children look to me to be perfect. When I do screw up they mentally put me straight into the 'bad parent' category.

One of my children has developed a different category (the other two are now starting to do the same). He has the ability to see me as a good parent who sometimes messes up. It's taken a long time to get there but it has really helped our relationship. This has come about in part through our discussions around the relationship glasses activity.

Every child I have ever done the activity with has essentially created a 'good parent' and a 'bad parent'. It shows their inability to see that even good people are capable of making bad choices or mistakes. And yet it is essential that they learn this. Being able to 'see the grey' will help them to not only accept our mistakes as parents, but also tolerate their own 'greyness'.

Believe and Your Child: A Summary

Your child's belief system is held in their thoughts, feelings, emotions, and bodily sensations. It is shown to you in their behaviour. We therefore need to explore those beliefs using different methods. Talking alone will not help if your child's difficult experiences happened at a time when they were not able to access their thinking brain. Not only do we need to support them to believe they are safe and lovable in regards to the thoughts they have about themselves and others, we also need to help them learn to calm their bodies, access their emotions and explore their feelings. Ideas about how to do this are given later in this book.

Questions To Ask.

Does my child believe they are physically, emotionally and socially safe?

Do they see themselves as lovable?

What might their relationship template look like?

How difficult might it be for them to change these beliefs?

13. Behave and Your Child

I'm going to take a guess that it was your child's behaviour that led you to pick up this book. What we have learned so far is that their behaviours are built upon the experiences of relationship that have left them believing that they are unsafe and/or unlovable.

As a therapist and trainer, I never get phone calls seeking my help for a child's beliefs. I get phone calls asking me to work with young people who show behaviours such as defiance, aggression, theft, absconding, disrespect and more. Often their family or school placements are at risk of breaking down. Parents and professionals always want to know if I can stop the behaviour and, if so, can I do it quickly. These questions are completely understandable, but they show a lack of understand about what behaviour is and how to work with it.

What is Behaviour?

On a very basic level, behaviour simply means the things we do. However, the things we do are informed by our thoughts, feelings, emotions and bodily sensations. As we have learned, these are informed by our experiences.

Behaviour is simply a child's beliefs in action. It is the way they show the outside world their inside world. Children who feel unsafe engage in safety behaviours and children who feel unlovable engage in shame behaviours.

The reason I get so many phone calls about behaviour is because it is how a child's belief system impacts other people. We take notice of a child's behaviour because of the effect it has not only on them but also on those around them, including ourselves. Many fostered and adopted children have a tendency to isolate themselves but I never get asked to work with them because taking yourself off to your bedroom for hours at a time is not usually seen as a problem behaviour.

What Are Challenging Behaviours?

What is challenging to someone else may not be challenging to you, and vice versa. This shows that our experience of a child's behaviour is very subjective. Sometimes I have found that other people really don't understand why I find a particular behaviour difficult.

For example, one of my children sings. He sings a lot. If he isn't singing then he's humming. If he isn't humming then he's talking. If I ask for a time of quiet then he will start muttering under his breath. For some people, being around constant noise isn't a problem. They actually really like it. I don't. I like quiet. If I'm in the house alone I will happily go about my business for several hours without the need for tv, radio or other sounds. I find that quiet recharges me. Some noise is fine but constant chatter drains me. I am much more likely to lose my temper over his singing than I am over bigger problem behaviours such as theft or deception.

Why Do Children Behave Like This?

Every behaviour your child engages in has a purpose. It is trying to communicate something to you. My son's constant noise is his way of saying to me 'Mum, don't forget I'm here'. On some level he believes that if he stopped being so noisy I might forget about him, and he'd rather get told off than have that happen.

Behaviour is usually how a child seeks confirmation of their relationship template. They will behave towards you as they have learned to behave in previous home environments. Those behaviours have often worked for them in the past. They have helped them to survive their previous parenting so they will naturally try and use the same behaviours to survive being parented by you.

So, when they feel unsafe physically, they will freeze, fight and flight. And when they feel unlovable and worry for their social safety they will attack, avoid and appease.

Can Children Control Their Behaviour?

Parent's often ask me how much control a child has over their behaviour. Actually, most parents do what I used to do and assume that the child is in complete control of what they do. I totally understand this. Like I said, I used to think the same way. I totally thought that my children could control their actions. When they stole from me I believed that they chose to do this. What they hit me I thought this was also a choice, and therefore something that they could chose not to do. The fact that they 'chose' these behaviours felt frustrating and upsetting to me.

Something that really helped me and has since been helpful to many young people and parents I work with, is Daniel Siegel's ideas about the Window of Tolerance.

The window of tolerance is basically how much stuff you can deal with and still feel ok. We are in our window of tolerance when our brains feel generally relaxed and not under threat.

When something happens that takes us out of our window of tolerance we either go above it or below it. If we go above then we become hyper-aroused. We go into a state of anxiety that triggers our fight and flight responses. If we go below then we are said to be hypo-aroused. This triggers our freeze response and is linked to low mood and depression.

We are all capable of becoming both hyper and hypo aroused but we will typically have a preference. I tend to go more towards depression when I am outside of my tolerance window. Knowing this helps me to be more aware and have a self-care plan in place.

If being outside our window of tolerance leads to us being anxious or depressed then we know that the part of the brain we will be most using at these times is our survival brain. Once again, our thinking brain is not really engaged. So, to answer the question of whether the child is in control of their behaviour, on the whole they are not. This is why, in the moment, reasoning with them doesn't work – they literally cannot access their thinking brains.

Behave and Your Child: A Summary

If it feels as though your child is behaving poorly a lot, then there is one clear reason for this: they have a very small window of tolerance. The size of everyone's window is different. In my experience, traumatised children have very, very small windows. This is because really bad things happened to them at a time when they had not developed the emotional resources to deal with it.

Part of our role as parents is to help them to grow their windows and become more resilient. As we do this we will find that they are less easily triggered and behaviours will improve.

Questions to Ask.

What does our child's behaviour achieve for them?

How does their behaviour fit with their relationship template?

What does their behaviour tell you about their beliefs?

How big is their window of tolerance?

Part 5

Belong, Believe, Behave: You & Your Child

So, here it is. The section you have been waiting for: the part where I tell you how to parent in a way that 'fixes' your child. I wonder how many people will have skipped straight to this part and not have read anything else. I'm not judging. I'm not in a place to do that, given that I did exactly the same with the first therapeutic parenting book I read.

I always think it's good to start to talk about parenting by first managing people's expectations. If you are looking for me to give you something along the lines of 'five easy ways to get your child to stop (insert difficult behaviour here)', then I'm afraid I will disappoint you.

Nothing about fostering and adoption is easy. For you, your child or those around you. Trauma is by definition difficult both in the moment and to recover from. There are no easy answers and I'm not going to promise you there are.

I think acknowledging this from the start is one of the most helpful things I can do for you. Too many times I have sat in training events and listened to people talk about parenting techniques in a way that suggests 'it's easy, you just do X and all the problems go away'. Often, I've gone home and one of two things has happened. I've put the technique in place and it has not had the desired effect or I've struggled to even do the technique at all. Either way, it's led to me feeling even worse about the situation I'm in or, more damagingly, it has further increased my sense of parental shame and hopelessness.

What I want to do in this section is not tell you what you need to do, but rather offer suggestions. I want to show you the basic principle of 3B's parenting and then give you lots of ideas for how you might apply it in practice. That way you can decide what is right for your child and for you.

14. 3B's Parenting: The Basic Principle.

Sometimes we talk about parenting traumatised children in a really complex way. I don't think that's helpful, especially when parents are already stressed. Therapeutic parenting is hard to do but the basic principle is something anyone can understand.

The most effective parenting for fostered and adopted children focuses on building a relationship that reduces fear and shame so that everyone feels safe enough and lovable enough.

That's it. Therapeutic parenting in one sentence. You can use any theory, method or technique so long as it is consistent with that principle. This allows you to completely tailor your parenting according to who you are, who your child is and the environment in which you are parenting. No two children are the same. They will all require different interventions. But all children, all people, do have the same need for safety and love. So, using this as my guide to choosing different techniques is what I have found to be the most helpful.

Time Out vs Time In Technique (Example).

I wanted to give you an example of how this principle works in practice and thought I would use the time out technique as an example.

Generally, the idea of giving a child a time out for poor behaviour is unhelpful. For many fostered and adopted children it triggers their issues with abandonment and isolation. Consequently, most people will tell you never to use it. However, I tend to be against the strict rules that are often given to parents (except obviously those that are illegal or could cause harm). I believe that every situation is different and there may be times when time outs are needed. It's often about how you use a technique rather than the technique itself.

To help, here is how this technique works (or doesn't) for my children.

Child 1.

He cannot bear time outs. They are simply too triggering for him. He struggles to manage any time alone at the best of times, let alone when he believes he's 'been naughty'. Time in's work for this child. That means that when he does something wrong or is struggling in any way we bring him in closer to us. It helps him to feel safe and loved as he doesn't fear disconnection from us. It doesn't take much time in close for him to then apologise for what he has done or talk about how he's feeling.

Child 2.

Child 2 cannot bear time ins when he has been caught doing something he shouldn't have. It's too triggering for him. He feels too ashamed and doesn't want anyone to see that shame. In that moment, attempts to get close to him result in fight and flight behaviours. We've learned to take a step back and give him space because this makes him feel safer. Technically he is having a self-enforced time out. If he doesn't reconnect with us then after a bit of time we will try to reconnect with him. If he's not ready then we will leave him until he is. We always do reconnect and he will now open up to us emotionally once he has taken time to calm down.

The time out makes him feel safer. Our attempts to reconnect make him feel loved. Eventually we'd love him to be able to stay with us 'in the moment' but presently he is not able to take what would for him be such a big relationship risk (that we would see his shame and reject him for it).

Child 3.

Child 3 just can't bear being in trouble. Full stop. Time outs would feel very abusive for him and he simply couldn't handle them. Bringing him in close is the better option. As soon as we do, this child likes to apologise and resolve as quickly as possible. A lot of the time this is fine. We talk and then we keep him close to ensure that he is ok.

Sometimes though he might be ready to talk, but I'm not. Sometimes I'm not feeling very loved or safe because of his behaviour. I feel cross and if I try to deal with that at that moment then I am likely to say something I later regret.

Sometimes his attempts to apologise and repair do not seem very genuine. There isn't true remorse. He's sorry he's in trouble rather than being sorry for what he has done. I struggle with this too. He might want me to forgive him quickly but sometimes that doesn't help him to learn or repair relationships properly and other times, well, I'm not feeling very forgiving.

The safest and most loving thing I can do in those moments is take a time out myself. The phrase 'Mum needs a cup of tea' has become synonymous with 'if you don't give me five minutes to myself I will lose my temper'! Child 3 knows that if he gives me this space then I will be able to engage with him in a safer way. He understands that it is because I love him that I want to get control of my emotions and not end up shouting at him.

So, as I hope I have shown, different children need different techniques to be used in different ways to meet their different love and safety needs. As parents we also need to engage in ways that feel safe and loving for us too.

15. The Two Methods of 3B's Parenting.

There is one basic principle to therapeutic parenting but there are lots of great ideas about how to put that principle into action. When examined together, it became clear to me that these techniques showed two different methods. I have called these The Relationship Method and The Response Method.

There is a reason why no-one can make a guarantee about the outcomes of their parenting model. That reason centres around power and control. We can control the interventions that we use with our children, but we can't control their response. Neither do we parent on a desert island. Our children are influenced by their environments and other relationships, much of which we have little influence over.

I think it's unhelpful therefore to parent in ways that only work if the child changes. Reward charts, for example, are usually unsuccessful with fostered and adopted children. Both the Relationship Method and the Response Method focuses on what is within your power to control regardless of how the child responds.

The next two sections of this book will explore these methods and the great techniques that they offer you and your child.

Part 6

The Relationship Method

The 3B's model shows the importance of the relationship between you and your child. It is through relationships that they have been most hurt and it is through a relationship with you that they will find healing. The Relationship Method is about providing the child with a relationship that gently challenges the safety and shame beliefs they hold so that the behaviours naturally begin to reflect this.

The key reason traditional parenting doesn't work for your child is that it assumes a good relationship exists already. My parents followed the traditional parenting of their time: they shouted at me, smacked me, sent me to my room etc. It did have a negative effect on me but it was tolerable because I held on to a belief that they did really love me and I felt safe enough with them. As a child, my relationship template was very different from the relationship template that my children have now.

The Relationship Method is about trying to re-create the 'normal' relationship experiences of children raised by loving parents. However, I want to be clear that this can be a very difficult thing to do. The natural process of parenting is to build a relationship with your baby and delight in them before having to deal with toddler behaviour. Foster and adoptive parents rarely have this option so have to deal with behaviour at the same time as trying to build the relationship.

The Relationship Method is proactive. It's hard, but it's in our control. As promised, here are some techniques that can be used with this method to meet the 3B's principle of building relationships that increase safety and reduce shame.

16. The Relationship Method and Belonging.

The whole premise of the relationship method is to encourage belonging. It offers the best possible opportunity for your child to attach to you and for you to bond to them. Let's consider some of the ways you might use the relationship method to do this.

You First.

The only thing that is within your power to change, is you. I'm going to be saying this a lot. In fact, you are going to get pretty annoyed with me about how much I go on about this.

One half of the relationship between you and your child is completely in your control. If there's one thing I know for sure, it's that your resources need to be good in order to meet the needs of your poorly resourced child.

You can't connect with your child if you have no love to give them, if you are stressed out, exhausted or depressed. None of us do relationships perfectly so where do you need to develop your relationship skills?

And for goodness sake, stop focusing everything on your child and give something to yourself each day – go for a walk, get as much sleep as you can, look after your thought processes, work through your emotions do what you need to do to feel safe and lovable. Your child will benefit from it in the long run.

Make the Relationship the Focus.

Easy to say but not so easy to do. Most of us find ourselves focusing on the behaviours for reasons I explained earlier in this book. We put a lot of energy into the wrong 'B'. If you change the behaviour, you will just end up creating a new one because the underlying belief system is still in place. That's why some people go from being a 'recovered' drug addict to other forms of addiction – the behaviour changes but it's still expressing the same underlying issues.

With some children, there are so many behavioural issues that parents find they have no time to deal with anything else. What this tells us is that these children feel far too unsafe and unlovable. The higher a child's behaviour needs are, the higher their need for a relationship that can contain them.

It's exhausting though, right? When my children's behaviour was at its worst it felt like I spent all day dealing with one crisis after another. If someone had asked me to then give more, my reaction to them would not have been very positive. I'm not going to ask you to give more. I'm going to ask you to be smart about what you give your energy to. You can only do so much. You cannot do it all, so don't expect that of yourself.

Try this activity. Make a list of all of the behaviours you find difficult from your child. Behaviour such as hitting, poor table manners or swearing. Add to it a list of behaviours they don't yet have but you would like to help them develop such as turn-taking, sharing or tidying their bedroom.

Is it a long list? Mine would have been.

Now take this list and designate each behaviour to one of the following categories:

1. Behaviours that are unsafe and definitely need to be dealt with every time.

2. Behaviours that are really unhelpful and need regular attention.

3. Behaviours that could be dealt with at a later point when my relationship with them is better.

4. Behaviours that I could learn to live with.

Only category one is essential. None of the other categories are more important than your relationship with your child. I'm not suggesting permissive parenting. Your child should not be allowed to behave however they like. All unhelpful behaviours should be acknowledged but think about how much of your time you give to managing them. A lot of the time it is enough to say "that behaviour is not acceptable because it hasn't made me feel very loved/safe" and leave it there. Repeating statements like these countless times a day will have an impact.

I guess it's a long-winded way of me saying focus on the big stuff (the relationship) and try not to sweat the small stuff.

Be A Role Model.

Children watch everything we do. This is especially true of traumatised children who are often constantly on 'danger alert'. What do you want your child to see when they are watching you?

I hate it when I tell one of my sons off for something only to realise that they have copied the behaviour from me. Sometimes my children are more like my mirror, reflecting back to me the parts of myself that are uncomfortable to acknowledge. To be honest, they have enough poor behaviours of their own, I really don't need them to pick up my bad habits as well!

Inevitably there will be times when your behaviour is not ideal. None of us are saints. It's ok for our children to see our 'messiness'. It's how we handle that that matters. I tell my children that there are parts of myself that I am still working on. If I need to I will always apologise to them. If I've been cross with my wife in front of them then I will apologise in front of them. If I need to do something to repair my relationship with them then I will do it.

One way of helping my children move away from seeking a 'perfect parent' has been to make it very clear that being perfect is unattainable – for them and for me.

Develop Attunement.

Attunement is when a parent knows what a child needs because they can connect to their internal world. It's not instinctive. If you watch a first-time parent of a new-born baby, you will see them spending a lot of time trying to work out why their child is crying – are they hungry? hot? cold? tired? wet? Etc.

For us foster and adoptive parents this is good news. It means we can develop attunement like a birth parent can. The bests way to do this is to try and see the world as your child would see it. A lot of trial and error and over time you may begin to see the subtle ways your child communicates their needs. Ways that they might not even be aware of. If I heard my son's tummy rumbling I would know that he was hungry. He had no sense of this because, although he was 10 years old, he didn't understand his bodily sensations. Being attuned and aware allowed me to meet his needs and thus strengthened my relationship with him.

I would argue that attunement of older children is more important for foster and adoptive parents than it is for birth parents. As most children get older they develop a good sense of what their needs are and are able to ask directly for those needs to be met.

A few years ago, I was having coffee with a friend and her daughter (aged 4) came and asked her for a banana. It was the most natural thing in the world and so my friend thought nothing of it. I told her that I wished my child could do that. She looked at me with disbelief. She was used to hearing me talk about the more extreme behaviours I dealt with every day, not the ability to ask for a banana.

My middle son adores bananas but at that point he would never ask me for one. His relationship template told him that parents say no all the time and let you go hungry. Instead he would look longingly at the fruit bowl until I would ask him if he wanted one. I had to be attuned to him or this need of his would not have been met.

His ability to ask for a banana is a small but significant thing that shows the progress he has now made. After a couple of years of longing looks, he started saying comments like "I like bananas". I would reply with "I know you do. Are you saying you would like to have one?". He'd say "yes" and I'd reply "Great, if you are hungry you can always ask". After several months of these conversations he then did start asking, but not for himself because the fear of a "no" was still too strong. "My brother would like a banana" he would say and of course he would receive one himself. The day he said "Mum, I'm hungry. Can I have a banana?" he received not only the fruit but a giant hug as well. He said I was "weird". I said I was proud of him and didn't care.

None of my children would have progressed to be able to ask for their needs (physical and emotional) to be met if we had not first learned to attune to them.

Know Everything You Can.

Attunement comes from knowing your child. In theory, foster and adoptive parents should know a lot about their children before they even come to live with them. In reality they often don't.

There was so much known about my children that was never told to us. Significant things. A couple of things that were intentionally withheld so that we would agree to take them into our home. There were things we found out when we came to adopt them that we hadn't been told in the eight years we'd fostered them. We are not alone in this.

If you are able to access files about your child then request to do so. Get the most information you can out of the professionals who have been involved in their life so far - they may not be able to share or even remember information at a later date. If they have siblings that are adopted or looked after then do their parents have any background information that might help you.

All of this information will benefit your child when it comes to life story work but it will really benefit you in deciding which techniques will be best to parent them with. The more you know the closer your relationship can become.

Surround Them with Helpful Relationships.

All of the work I did to help my son feel safe in school was quickly undone by one supply teacher. I got a phone call to come to school because he 'had been incredibly rude and disobedient'. As you can imagine, I raced up to the school with all kinds of scenarios playing in my head. My son was 8 years old at the time and I spent so much time up at that school I had my own mug in the staffroom!

When I arrived, he was sat meekly outside the headteachers office. I checked he was ok and went to speak to the teacher who had called me. She told me that during an English lesson he had become insistent that a particular word existed. She had said that it didn't. He'd left his seat to go and get a dictionary. She ordered him to stay sitting down. He got the dictionary anyway. She tried to take it off him but he wouldn't let her have it. He found the word and started to read out what it meant. She told him to leave the room. He refused. She told him he was disrespecting her. He told her that she was disrespecting his knowledge! She 'used her big voice' and then he ran out of the classroom 'to show her he could do what he wanted'.

I told her that her 'big voice' would have been interpreted as shouting by my son and it would make him anxious. I doubted he had run out of the classroom as an act of defiance but more likely because his flight mechanism had been triggered.

I asked her if she had apologised to him and I tell you, if looks could kill I would be 6ft under! She asked me why she would do that. As politely as possible (given my ever-growing frustration with her) I reminded her that my son had been right. The word did exist. I suggested she apologise for her part in what happened and that if the same things happened again (as it likely would) she invite my son to get a dictionary and show her what he knows. She told me that she had never apologised to a student and was not going to start now. She felt this would 'undermine her authority'.

She asked me what I was going to do about his rudeness. I told her that I wouldn't expect him to apologise when the adult in the situation was unwilling to do the same. I did however say I would praise him for his intelligence but suggest better ways of letting people know how clever he was.

I would have loved to be in the staffroom later that day!

The reality is that this lady was poorly trained. Sadly, as I write this book, most child-related professionals in the UK have had none or very little training about children like ours. I have spent a lot of time as a parent educating the other adults around my sons. Much of this was done before I later trained as a therapist. Some professionals have been very resistant to listening to a parent. However, I cannot underestimate the impact that other adults can have on your child. That impact can be very positive or very negative. I believe the time I have invested in 'getting them on side' has paid dividends in the long term.

Relationship Education.

Being in a relationship with someone involves certain social skills. Skills your child may be lacking. They might have other skills for relationships such as charming, manipulating or bullying, but these are hardly going to set them up for healthy relationships in the future.

We need to educate our children about how relationships work. They need to understand that they are supposed to be to the benefit of both people and they need to do things like share, take turns, agree boundaries together etc. We do all of this normally with a toddler. Your 14-year-old many need to learn the same lessons.

As well as teaching them what relationships are, we need to teach them what they aren't. In sensitive and loving ways, we need to uphold that the experience of relationships they have previously had weren't right. You may be able to do this in a direct way with your child. It will depend on their ongoing feelings and relationship with their birth parent. The indirect technique is to gently challenge by making comments that encourage the child to reach their own conclusions.

Spend Time with Your Child.

This may seem like an obvious one but I'm writing it down because there are definitely times when the last thing I want to do with my children is spend more time with them. When things are hard, it can be as easy for us to ty to avoid them as it is for them to want to avoid us.

But 1-1 time is so important. If, like me, you are parenting more than one child, then I would encourage you to think about where in your day you are able to give each child quality, undivided attention. There are professionals who have come up with formulas according to a child's age about how often they need this time and for how long. If this helps you, then fantastic. Personally, I find if I engage with my children according to a timetable then it becomes a chore rather than something I want to do. And that doesn't put me in the right frame of mind for good relationship building. My personal goal is to find a way to connect with each child every day. Sometimes I might do something with them for a full day. Other days they might only get 10 minutes. But if 10 minutes of quality time is all I can manage that day then it's better than nothing. I'm not in the habit these days of trying to live up to unrealistic expectations.

17. The Relationship Method and Safety Beliefs

It is through past relationship that our children have been most unsafe. But where there is hurt is often where there is the greatest potential for healing. Through a relationship with you, your child's safety beliefs can be gently challenged and changed. Let's consider some techniques to do this.

You First.

Your child can only feel as safe as you do. With that in mind, we know that you must meet your safety needs before you can truly meet your child's. I hope that in the earlier section, when we explored what the 3B's means for you, you were able to identify your safety needs. I hope too that you were able to consider the difference between being safe and feeling safe.

I know that when my children's behaviour has been the riskiest, I have often felt unsafe. Sometimes I have over-estimated the risk prompting me to respond to them from fear instead of love. Sometimes I have underestimated the risk or not been willing to truly admit how I feel. Often this has been because acknowledging it brings questions such as, 'Can he still live here?' And, as a mum who loves her children, those questions are scary in themselves.

I know that to parent my children best, I must feel safe enough. Safe in thoughts, feeling and bodily sensations. For that reason, it is not only my children who have a safer care plan. I have written one for myself too. It includes lots of things I can do to feel safe enough and good enough. One of the things that I am absolutely clear on is that experiences that are unsafe must be worked through.

When I was a foster parent we had to report any significant events or concerns. Out of normal working hours this meant calling an emergency number. Most of the time I would speak to someone who would ask for details, log it, ask me to write a report and discuss how the information would be passed on or how the situation would best be handled. There was one woman though who didn't do this. When I called her following a difficult incident, she asked me to go and take 30 minutes, have a cup of tea (we are British after all!) and then ring her back. When I did call back, her first question was not about my children, or what had happened. It was simple "How are you?".

So, my advice to managing your safety needs is simple. When something scary happens, ask yourself "how are you?" and then follow it up with "and what do you need?". Then make time to get those needs met.

Meet Their Basic Needs.

None of us feel safe if our basic needs for food, water, shelter and warmth aren't met. It seems obvious to say that you need to meet these needs but our children can be very poor at communicating their needs, or even knowing what they are. As I have already said, developing attunement with your child is so incredibly beneficial.

Many of us are also parenting children who, in some areas, are very capable. Children who have learned to meet their own needs themselves. When my eight-year-old told me he could cook a full English breakfast, I didn't believe him. But he could, and he did. He hated us hoovering because he felt this was his job. He would happily stack the dishwasher and empty it. In fact, he would happily spend all day cleaning and tidying. It was really tempting to allow him to continue to do these jobs (my house was looking very clean!). But I knew that the boy who could dust the furniture like a pro, couldn't play with Lego or ride a bike. There were child skills he hadn't developed because of the pseudo-maturity he displayed.

I also knew that he had learned to do these things because he had not experienced a relationship with a parent who was willing to do them for him. My son needed to understand that his basic needs could be met by a parent who loved him and wanted to care for him.

Your child may not be a child. They may be very quickly approaching adulthood. There might be lots of discussion about their need to be independent. However, their need for a parent who makes them feel safe will always be greater. So maybe you could still cook for them occasionally? Or how about doing laundry together? Could tidying the house become a family activity? I know the thought of them being independent is a happy one for most of us, but the truth is that we can never really learn independence if we haven't learned to be dependent in the first place.

Know Their Triggers.

What is it that makes your child most scared? When you have the answer to this question, there is so much you can do to minimise the chances of them needing to freeze, fight or flight. It's likely that your child is not aware enough or lacks the emotional language to explain what their fear is. For that reason, an attitude of curiosity is really helpful. When difficult situations occur, it is always helpful to reflect on them afterwards and wonder what the trigger was. Sometimes the trigger is obvious, sometimes it's harder to work out and sometimes it's so small that it's nearly impossible to detect. But if you can find it then you are able to build a relationship with your child that either avoids that trigger or supports them to be better able to manage it in the future.

Appropriate Boundaries.

When I was a teenager those caring for me would often say things like, "If you are going to behave like a three-year-old then I'm going to treat you like a three-year-old". Sound familiar to anyone? Well, I'm going to say to you that if your ten-year-old acts like a three-year-old, it's mostly likely because they actually are three years old. Trauma at a young age causes developmental delay. Your child may be cognitively capable but emotionally struggling. It doesn't help any child to treat them at their chronological age if they didn't have chance to develop their life skills when they were younger.

Our children need boundaries that help them to feel safe. Those boundaries need to be developmentally appropriate rather than age appropriate. Understandably, many foster and adoptive parents feel caught between letting their children do what other children their age do or letting them do what they can manage to do. Often those who don't understand view us as either too controlling or over-protective as a result.

So, if your child is operating at a much younger level, it is best to give them the boundaries of a much younger child. This usually means really high supervision to help them make good choices. It means helping them to structure their time and activities. It means constantly assessing and managing risk until they are able to do this for themselves. It means maintaining a safe environment that minimises the risks for them

If you do this, then you will find that as the child feels safer with you, you will be able to slowly reduce the boundaries around them. This of course is exactly what birth parents do as children get older and so you are following a natural parenting process. It is just, like most things in fostering and adoption, harder because of the lack of initial trust the child has in your parenting.

Safety Language

This is one of the most powerful techniques I use.

Children who have a trauma history don't often have a clear understanding of safety. They don't know what it feels like. They can't put words to it. They don't understand what makes them feel safe or what safety might feel like for other people. So, we have to educate them.

For me, this started with a more general approach towards increasing their emotional literacy. Every day after school we would sit down for a snack and have 'feelings time'. Just as with very young children, my sons (9, 10 and 12yrs at the time) could only recognise the emotions of happy, sad and angry. They had no other emotional language.

They also struggled to be truly honest about the emotions they experienced. My eldest reported that he was continually happy. I remember an occasion when his brother had hit him hard in the stomach. He was crying uncontrollably and I asked him how he was feeling, "happy" he replied.

We need permission to express our emotions. We need to know that it's ok to be sad and it's ok to be angry. It's what we do with those difficult feelings that matters. We have a lot of unhelpful messages around feelings in our culture. Anger is seen as a male characteristic not acceptable for women, whereas it is acceptable for girls to cry but not for boys. These are issues that tend to affect all people, but for children with trauma histories the issues around emotional expression run much deeper.

I wonder what happened to your child in the past if they became upset? Maybe they were told to "get over it and stop being a wimp". Maybe they'd get a slap from Mum or maybe they were simply ignored and left in their distress. Whatever their experiences, the emotions they learned to deny are inside them, often bubbling away at the surface. If we give them permission to express them verbally or creatively (through art, writing etc) then they are much less likely to need to express them behaviourally.

So, we started where they were at. Every day we asked them to name experiences that had made them feel happy, sad or angry. We also shared our experiences. Over time we were able to add in other emotions until our children had a very good emotional language.

We also talked a lot about the emotional boundaries to our relationships. Once a child understands how they feel then they are able to begin to develop empathy for how other people feel. If they can't do the first then they can't do the latter. We spent a long time discussing the emotion they all felt was most unsafe for them: anger. We used emotional language to explain emotional intensity and what was and wasn't acceptable in our family. We talked about how we might feel cross or angry with their behaviours but we would never, ever, feel rage towards them. Anger is the feeling that lets us know that someone's behaviour is unsafe or unlovable. Rage is anger out of control and is not a part of a loving and safe family.

Alongside the emotional literacy work we began to use safety language. We only had one family rule – 'Treat everyone and everything safely and lovingly' – and would relate everything back to this. When discussing poor behaviour, we would highlight its safety risks. When going to new places we would discuss a safety plan. Consequences were given to "help you learn to be safe". We used the word 'safe' so often that if I use it now, ten years on, my children roll their eyes at me in a typical teenager 'I know it all already' fashion!

They might have gotten fed up with me saying it, but there's a reason why we used the word so much. Our children, and I suspect your children, always presumed the worse of us. Those very frustrating relationship templates of theirs did not allow for a parent who made rules and decisions based on a desire to keep everyone safe. My children usually believed that my motive was to control them, to stop them having fun or to punish them in some way.

We had to get good at explaining our actions to them. Left to their own devices, they would jump to conclusions of their own. Those conclusions were never right and usually unhelpful. Phrases like "I'm saying this because…" or "I did that because…" became common place in our home. And those phrases always related our decisions and actions back to the themes of safety and love.

Safety language is very powerful. It stops a child from having to guess how you are feeling and what your motives are. Again, they will likely test it out but once it is clear to them that what you say is true, behaviours tend to naturally start to improve.

Increase Their Window Size

Remember those small windows of tolerance? Well, as parents we can use our relationships to teach and support our children to make them bigger. This is partly through role-modelling how we build our own resilience but also through teaching and guiding.

There is nothing that I am writing in this book that you can't educate your child about. It may have to be done sensitively but it can be hugely beneficial. I am a big believer in providing people with education so that they can better understand themselves. The children's stories I have written and the concept of the Brain Switches are aimed at helping young people understand in simple ways how their brains function, why they might not be able to do what their peers can and the defences they may be using against shame.

For me, learning about why my children do what they do has given me a great opportunity to better understand myself too. I'm definitely less critical of my behaviour knowing that it is something to be curious about instead.

Engaging in activities that teach them to care for themselves will increase their internal resources and make them more capable of dealing with difficult people and situations. Cognitive knowledge is really good for some children but I personally find the best techniques lie in working with the body more than the mind.

Until children are able to make sense of their trauma it is usually held in the body. This is why their bodies can be triggered in freeze, fight and flight so easily. We have to help our children feel that their bodies are safe and learn how to relax them. Children are not designed for sitting for long periods of time either at school or in front of the tv. They need to be active. They need to run, jump, swing, climb, skip, bend and hop.

They also need to learn to feel within their bodies. Children who have been physically or sexually hurt often learn to 'cut off' from their physical feelings. Their bodies feel unsafe for them. Practices such as mindfulness, body scanning, deep breathing and yoga can really help them to reengage and begin to feel safe again.

You as a Safety Figure.

In a loving home, birth children come to see their parents as safety personified. In time, I hope that your children will come to see you in the same way.

To feel safe with you, your children need to know that you are in control. Being in control is not the same as being controlling. A parent in control feels safe, a controlling parent doesn't.

Your child firstly needs you to be in control of yourself – your thoughts, feelings, bodily sensations and how they show in your behaviour.

They likely need you to be in control of decision making. Traumatised children find decision making very difficult.

They may need you to initially make the majority of decisions or limit their options down to a small number they can cope with.

What they don't need is to be in control of everything themselves. Many fostered and adopted children will battle for power and control. At times it may feel like it would be much easier to let them have it. I get it, the battles can be exhausting. But if your child was to truly have the level of power that they might appear to want, it would actually make them feel incredibly unsafe. No matter how your child appears, they know deep down that they cannot maintain their own safety on their own. They need you.

If you are your child's safety figure then let's also consider what happens for them at times when you are not available.

Separation anxiety is very common for babies and toddlers. If you have ever been to a nursery on the first day of a new year you will usually see very young children crying as their parents walk out of the playground. A lot of fostered and adopted children experience this same anxiety when temporary separated from their parents too. I've often worked with teenagers who struggle at school simply because their mum or dad isn't there.

The first approach to managing this is to be clear about what the fear is. The fear of the separation is that it will be permanent. This is especially true of those young people who no longer have any contact with their birth families or who have had multiple placement moves.

So, how can you help your child to understand that this separation is temporary? Well, I find a couple of techniques really help. Firstly, I am very clear on the timing of my return. I will always give myself a bit of leeway (say 10 minutes or so) to ensure that I do return when I say I will. Secondly, I talk to them a lot about future events. If I'm leaving them with a babysitter on a Saturday night then I will make sure they know that I have plans to spend time with them on Sunday. This reassures them more if I can talk excitedly about how much I am looking forward to whatever it is I'm planning on doing with them.

Finally, and most helpfully, I use transition objects. These are objects that will remind my child of me and that he knows I need him to return to me when he sees me again. For three years my eldest son went to school every day with a hanky of mine. He knew that it was his job to look after it and that I would like it back but also that nothing bad would happen should he accidentally misplace it.

The hanky was sprayed with my perfume. For the first 6 years of parenting I chose to only wear one fragrance so that they would associate that smell with me. My son's teachers reported that they knew when he was struggling with something because he would take his hanky out and start sniffing it. The smell felt safe to him and became one of his coping strategies.

Prepare for Difficulties.

One thing I was completely unprepared for as a new parent was how long it may take for some of my children's behaviours to change. It seemed that so many of the things they did were really unhelpful to them and so I just couldn't get my head around why they continued to do them. I felt as though I was having the same conversations on repeat. The long summer holiday felt like six weeks of groundhog days. And my feelings seemed to endlessly sway between hope and disappointment.

Of course, now that I understand how the 3B's work, I know that my children won't give up their survival strategies easily. I also know that it's their safety beliefs that I need to challenge and the best way I can do this is by providing them with a safe relationship.

I know all of that. I teach all of that. I've spent months writing all of that for you to know too. But sometimes there is a big distance between what I know and what I feel. Every time I talk to one of my children about their behaviour I hope it will be the last time, but I no longer live my life as though it will be.

They say 'hope for the best and prepare for the worst'. This is great advice for parents of children with difficult experiences. I find preparing for the behaviour to happen again helps to keep my expectations realistic. And when I'm realistic about what my children may do, I'm much less disappointed when they do it.

Preparing for the worst for me means 'if-then' thinking. 'If this happens, then I will do this'. 'If my son engages in this behaviour, then this will be the consequence'. 'If my child is struggling in the supermarket then I will leave with them and get food delivered'. 'If I feel too unsafe then I will step back'. If, if, if, if, if. Then, then, then, then, then.

The benefit I find in thinking this way (other than managing my disappointment levels) is that I am prepared with a clear plan. A plan I hope I will not have to use but a plan none-the-less. Previously, I have asked you to list your child's behaviours. Now I would ask to you come up with an 'if-then' plan for each one you are working with. Doing this puts you in a position of being proactive instead of reactive. The plan will likely need to be reviewed each time you implement it but then you will have a better idea for what may work in the future.

I generally share my 'if-then' plans with my children. In fact, we often come up with them together now. Doing this makes me a more predictable parent for them – of course they do often need to test out that I will do what I say! A consistent parent is always better than an inconsistent one. Meaning what you say and saying what you mean is so very important.

I also spend a lot of time with them developing their own plans. One of my sons is a runner, and I don't mean in a healthy, enters lots of races, kind of way. He is very easily triggered into flight. Over the years the frequency of such events has significantly decreased and when he does run he doesn't tend to do so for long anymore.

I'll be honest, when triggered he is fast, very fast and I stand no chance of running after him. So, we have a very clear if-then plan. If he becomes aware that he has run away from me then he can return and I will give him a hug. He won't be told off but we may need to talk about what happened and how we can try to avoid him running in the future.

He used to run several times a day and could be gone for long periods. He wouldn't come back because he feared the adult's response and so we would have to try and find him. In the past year, my son has been triggered into flight twice. He has followed this plan every time, always returning within a few minutes.

18. The Relationship Method and Love Beliefs

Shame is the belief that you are not lovable. The fear associated with this is rejection, isolation and disconnection. Therefore, I would argue, that it is only through relationship that a person's sense of shame can diminish.

You First.

What does being lovable mean to you? How might that impact your relationship with your child? You've had a little time now since reading those early chapters, so in what ways have you put self-nurture into action?

You need to have love to give love. It starts with you. So, in the politest way possible, go love yourself.

Get the Nurture Level Right

The level of boundaries your child needs to keep them safe is the same level of nurture they require too. So, if like most traumatised children, they need a lot of supervision, structure and clear rules then they also need a lot of loving messages, affection and care. Boundaries on their own can quickly become, or at least appear to be, punitive. Nurture is what allows us to provide for the child's safety needs without increasing their sense of shame.

This is, of course, really hard to do. Constantly supporting a child to make good choices and keep themselves and others safe is exhausting. We can easily become frustrated and angry with them. The more we do that, the more we strengthen their negative view of themselves and the worse the behaviour becomes.

For me, the best approach has been to continually keep in mind that behaviour is only a way my children communicate. If a baby gets hungry and cries I would accept that. I would not think they were behaving badly. So, when my 14yr old gets hungry and becomes moody, I try to address this in the same way. Giving him a hug and a sandwich is how I metaphorically pick him up, soothe him, and meet his need.

Children who have had a lack of nurture will typically respond one of two ways to you. Some children will seek it continually. Any amount of nurture you give them will seem not enough. They are like a two-year-old continually clinging to Mummy or Daddy. One of my boys had to be in constant physical connection with me from the moment he got up until he went to bed. If I went to the bathroom he would try to join me. When he couldn't he would sit outside the door and need me to talk to him continually. This was somewhat problematic for me given that I had only gone to the bathroom for a bit of peace in the first place! The fear for him was that he had to get the nurture whilst he could because he believed it would end.

Other children will reject the parent's attempt to provide loving care. For months another of my children (then aged 8yrs) told me that he would never give me a hug, never call me 'Mum' and didn't want me to do anything for him, ever.

For him, the issue was the same. He didn't trust that the nurture would last. He didn't trust our motives for wanting to provide it and he felt the need to protect himself from it. Imagine the pain he would feel if he let us get that close to him, if he let his guard down and we then rejected him in anyway.

It is hard to accept nurture if you don't believe you are worth nurturing. That has been a consistent theme throughout all my work with fostered and adopted young people. It is truly sad to see a young person who has been hurt by the adults who should have cared for them now not be able to accept the nurture of adults who so desperately do love them.

As parents we can't control the responses our children make to us. All that is within our control is the option to continue to offer them the love and care we believe they are worthy of.

Age Appropriate Nurture.

Just as safety needs need to be met at the child's functioning age, so to do nurture needs.

One of the best pieces of advice we received was to have toys in our house that were suitable for a wide range of ages. We found that as soon as we did this, our children stopped engaging with toys aimed at their chronological age and began playing with toys for infants and toddlers.

From that basis we began to look at what other activities were appropriate to significantly younger children and test out whether our boys might also enjoy them. This is how I ended up every night bottle feeding and swaddling a 10, 11 and 14yr old as part of a 'Mummy time' routine. Yes, you read that right. Without any hesitation my children would climb onto one of our laps, drink their milk, get wrapped in a blanket and enjoy a bedtime story. We also had great fun with dressing up, sing-a-longs, puppet shows, blanket forts, bath-time toys, blowing bubbles and more.

Those experiences were really significant for my children and helped them to not only get closer to us but also to reach some of their developmental milestones. We were providing them with nurturing activities that filled the gaps in their experiences. We were allowing them to be the children they had not had chance to be. For a lot of fostered and adopted children these gaps don't really begin to be met until much later in life, if at all. Usually it is the case that their own need for nurture really begins to be met through nurturing their own children. I say let's not let them wait that long. Let's let them be infants, toddlers and children now.

Nurture Them Daily

You likely need to discipline your chid daily, so it's important that you nurture them daily too. There are many ways to nurture a child and different children will enjoy nurture in different ways. Some really like to be touched. They love hugs, high-fives and hand massages. Some like to hear you say you love them or find little notes inside their lunchboxes. Some like it when you do things for them or when you both do something nice for someone else together. Others may like you to do an activity with them or spend time chatting about their day. Some like receiving little gifts. They don't have to be expensive, they just have to show them that you care.

All of these ways that we show our children we love them help them to feel that they belong and, to someone at least, they are lovable.

Fun Experiences.

Quality time with our children also allows us to build memories as we share in fun experiences together. Sadly, this was one of the first things I stopped doing in the early days. The relationship template in my head said that if a child is behaving disrespectfully towards their parent then they didn't get to have nice times. Why should I take them swimming when an hour ago the dinner I lovingly made for them got thrown at the wall? Why should they get to go to the park to play when I've spent most of the morning painting over the penis they drew on their brother's bedroom wall? The underlying thought is: why should I treat them nicely when they don't do the same to me?

I know I'm not the only one to think like this. I hear it from parents all the time. It's completely understandable. I wonder what would have happened to you as a child if you had treated your parents the way your child treats you. I'm guessing you wouldn't have had a fun trip out and been bought nice things.

But making nice memories with your child is not about rewarding their behaviour. It's about saying "even though you do what you do, I still love you and want to spend time with you". Their behaviour might not deserve it, but who they are as a person certainly does.

Having fun times amongst the difficulties has been a significant factor in my children being able to move from feelings of shame to feelings of guilt. They understand very clearly that I love them, I just don't like some of the things they do.

You may find at the start that even these fun experiences need to be kept short and easy to manage. Most children with high levels of shame will feel that they don't deserve this special attention and try to self-sabotage your efforts to enjoy each other's company.

Set them Up to Succeed.

Shame and failure go hand in hand. Even those of us with really good self-worth many struggle in situations where we feel we have failed. Failure is almost guaranteed to trigger thoughts of not being good-enough. Where some of us can bounce back and learn from those situations, most of our children cannot. Failure for them is crushing. It only serves to confirm the negative views they hold of themselves.

We can't prevent a child from feeling like a failure. But we can help them not to fail. We can think about the situations we place them in and whether or not they can really handle them. We can be realistic in our expectations of them and not try and get them to be more than they are capable of being.

Separate Who They Are from What They Do.

I've called my son 'a stupid boy' on more than one occasion. I'm not proud of it, I'm just saying. Most of us know that we need to separate the child from their behaviour but it's easier to say than it is to do. Children can still feel unlovable when we attack their behaviour but they are much more likely to feel it when we use language that attacks who they are.

If we are aiming to move them from unhealthy shame to healthy guilt then we need to model this in the ways we speak about their behaviour.

Let Them Be Who They Are.

Young children are often given a lot of freedom to just be. To be who they are and be celebrated for doing so. We delight in their funny ways, their blossoming personalities and all the things that make them who they are.

Then we start to change all that. We start to focus on making them acceptable to society, to our friends, our family and to their schools. Whilst some of this may be necessary to create a safe and loving society, much of it is not. We send lots of messages to our children about who they need to be to be lovable. As they adapt to these messages they begin to lose a lot of their identity in the process.

The search for authenticity is a struggle that a lot of adults experience. Who am I if I am not being who I have been told I need to be? If I am the real me will I be accepted or is it better to remain this other person and stay connected? I'm sure that many of us can identify with this.

So, let's try not to pass our shame on to the next generation. Let's encourage our children to be safe, loving and their authentic self. Let's not seek society's ideals of perfection but instead celebrate what makes our children who they are. And whilst we are at it, let's do that for ourselves as well.

Catch Them Being Good

Traditional reward charts don't usually work with our children. That's because the success of them rests with the child and too many fostered and adopted children will self-sabotage any good results they achieve. They also focus too much on changing the behaviour rather than understanding it.

'Catch them being Good' is a great alternative. It means you can still reward good behaviour but you remain entirely in control of it. It's very simple, you just keep an eye out for anything they do that you want to encourage them to keep doing. Then you immediately reward it. This could be with a big hug or a small gift.

We solved settling for bed with this tactic. When we caught them being good they received a marble that went in a jam jar. We told them that once the jar was full we'd go for a big day out to a local theme park. We randomly gave out the marbles so that they generally couldn't work out how to manipulate the system. They realised that with each of them able to receive marbles then they were best to work together and support each other to make good choices. As the biggest issue at this time was their behaviour at bedtime, they quickly realised that settling for bed properly was likely to earn them the most marbles. They thought they were manipulating us to get what they wanted but by the time we had our trip out they were settled into a bedtime routine that continued from then onwards. Win, win!

Speak Love

You know that the decisions you make for your child are because you love them but they might not understand this. Just as we need to speak the language of safety, we also need to speak the language of love. We need to explain our motives to them rather than leaving them to come to their own conclusions. Some of us might be very comfortable with talking about love, others might not. Many families don't. Love is understood but not spoken. This may be an area of personal growth for you in order to meet the needs of your child.

Let Them Speak Shame

It's really uncomfortable to hear a child speak shame. When they talk about hating themselves it's all too easy to rush in with comments such as "you shouldn't think like that". When they tell you they are ugly, it's easy to find yourself disagreeing and saying "no you're not, you're beautiful" or "everyone's beautiful in their own way". When they tell you they are stupid, it's easy to start listing all the evidence that proves otherwise.

But what are we really doing in those moments? Our children don't hear the messages we are trying to convey, they hear that we don't really know them. We don't know how terrible they really are. Then they consciously or unconsciously decide to either show us their 'terribleness' or hide it away. Alternatively, they hear that we are lying to them and it only confirms that they can't trust us.

In that moment your child was opening up to you. They were trusting you with their deepest feelings. If they are open then we want to keep them that way. It's painful for us to hear their words but it's much more painful for them to feel it and not be able to express it.

When people speak shame, we must avoid our tendency to correct them. Although well intentioned, it is unhelpful. Instead we need to sit with their pain and allow them the space to fully express it. We can then empathise with how difficult it must be for them to feel the way they do. Only once we have allowed the shame a voice can we share that we see them differently – but still we must allow them to see themselves however they wish.

Find Something You love.

I heard Psychotherapist Daniel Hughes make this suggestion not long after my crying on the stairs moment. I found it really helpful so I'm sharing it with you now. He advised finding one thing that you love about your child and holding on to that one thing through the difficult times. For some children you may be able to list many lovable qualities. For other children you may struggle to think of one. One of my sons had a beautiful smile. It lit up his face. It was rarely seen and so I made it my mission to try and get him to smile every day. I didn't always manage it but I was able to hold on to the image of that smile none the less.

For children I work with and don't know well or those who do everything they can to push people into not loving them, the thing I hold onto is their struggle. I love them for the story of their life, the experiences that have bought them to where they are now. I love them for their ability to survive.

As a therapist I am often told that I should not love my clients. It is considered by many to be unprofessional. But I do love them. I've been able to love every client I have ever worked with whether child, parent or another professional. In fact, I won't work with someone that I can't love. I figure that enough of my clients have been hurt from being in loveless relationships. I won't become another. This is true for your child too.

Part 7

The Response Method

19. Why We Need The Response Method

In terms of parenting, my preference will always be for the relationship method. That's because it's the option that the parent has the most control over. It's proactive and can be thought through and implemented according to a plan.

But let's be honest here. No matter how amazing a parent you may be, there will be times when your child doesn't respond to you. There will be times when situations and experiences outside of your control lead to your child thinking, feeling and therefore behaving in unhelpful ways. Many of these times will occur with no warning and no chance to be prepared.

I am also aware that in the early stages of fostering and adopting, most of us find ourselves parenting without the relationship. Birth parents have a couple of years of bonding with their children before having to manage behavioural issues. Many of us haven't had that luxury. We often are having to deal with significant behavioural difficulties from our children whilst simultaneously trying to build a relationship with them.

I'd love to say, focus everything on the relationship but if I'd done that, well, at least two of my children would have died on multiple occasions. I had to put boundaries in place to keep them safe but my children's perception was that I was doing this to control them and stop them having fun. Our need to keep them safe can be to the determent of our relationships with them in the short term.

The relationship method uses a top-down method. It focuses on building a relationship that gently challenges the child's beliefs and naturally impacts their behaviours. I believe it is the best option overall but I want to offer you a model that reflects the fact that you may not have a great relationship with your child at the moment.

The response method uses a bottom-up method. It responds to the child's behaviour so as to challenge the beliefs and improve the relationship. It can be used with the child that you are struggling to connect with as well as the one you have only just met. The purpose of the response method is to allow you to address poor behaviour in a way that makes building a good relationship more likely.

In the early days of therapeutic parenting my children's behaviour meant I was using the response method a lot! In time though our relationships were built and the need for me to respond to their behaviour in this way decreased. Happy days!

To explain this further, allow me to tell you a part of the 3B's model I haven't yet included in this book.

20. The 3B's Cyclical Effect.

Our beliefs start to be formed from our experiences in relationship but over time another factor comes into play: our behaviours. Our behaviours begin to either challenge or reinforce the beliefs that we hold. All behaviours serve a purpose. If they don't then we may try them out once and never do them again. Your child's behaviour may seem to be really unhelpful to them but there is a reason they are doing it. They are gaining something from it. In some way it is supporting the beliefs they hold around how to survive this world and how they see themselves.

How we respond to their behaviours can either support or challenge their beliefs. In turn that can change or sustain how they are in relationship with us.

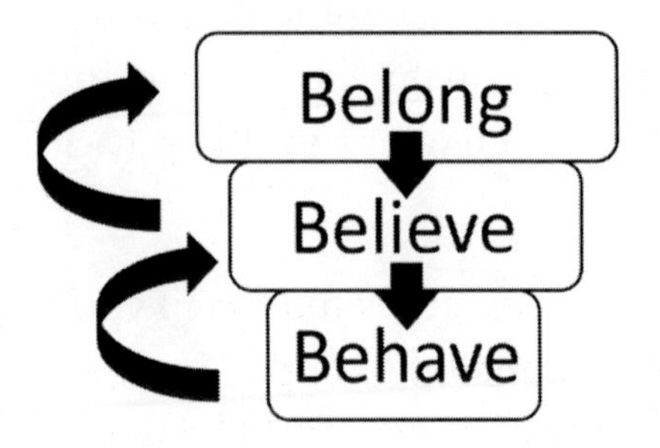

Let me share an example with you that I frequently encounter in my work. I am often working with young people who are triggered into a fight response in a school setting. Something feels unsafe for them and so they lash out. Sometimes towards other pupils, sometimes towards property and occasionally towards staff. Currently in the UK there is a significant lack of training around trauma for those working in an educational setting. What typically happens is that the child is restrained by staff. The child will likely experience this as a loss of control through being overpowered. This will feel unsafe for them and reinforce their beliefs about engaging in relationships with adults, especially authority figures.

This can become a vicious cycle.

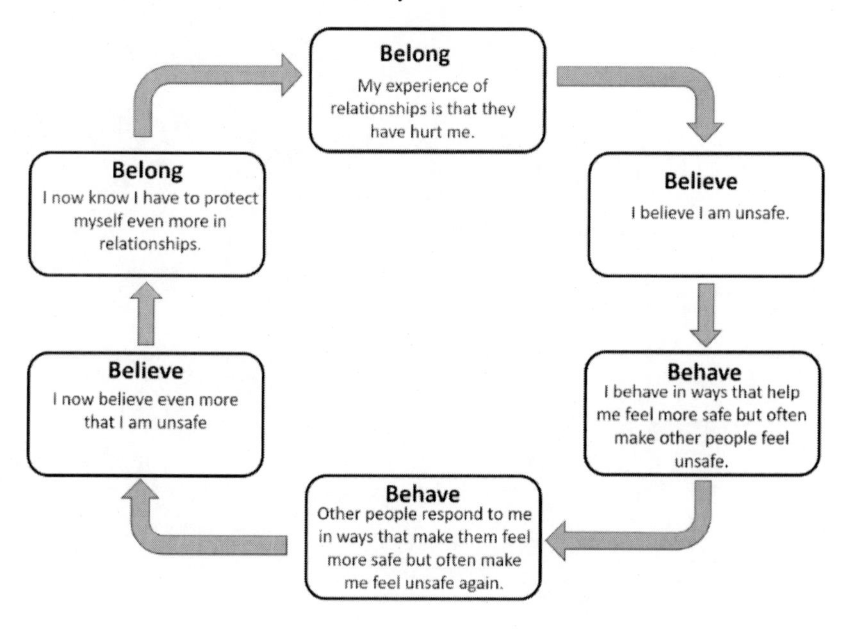

What this does tell us, though, is that how we respond to a child's behaviour has the power to change their safety and shame beliefs. This is what I call the Response Method.

The Response Method is reactive. You can plan for how you will respond to certain behaviours but in the moment, following through on those plans, is not always so easy. The Response Method uses many of the same techniques of the

Relationship Method however, there is a need for a much stronger focus on relationship repair.

21. The Response Method and Belonging.

You might not have a good relationship with your child, but how you respond to their behaviour can be part of the answer to getting one. Responses to their behaviour in the past will have been unhelpful (which is why they still engage in that behaviour). You can offer them something different. Here's some ideas for how to do that.

You First.

One of my biggest criticisms of therapeutic parenting books is that they don't tend to address what you do in the moment. There is lots of great, helpful advice about putting in plans around the child but never really much about that split second in which you become aware of your child's poor behaviour.

So, here is what I recommend: you breathe. Unless your child is at imminent risk then your first focus is not on them but on yourself. You pause. You pause for as long as it takes for you to gather yourself and calm yourself enough to reduce any intense emotional reactions you may have. The length of time this takes will differ from situation to situation.

Connect.

Once you have calmed yourself, your next step is attunement. What does your child need? Yes, they need to know that whatever they have done is wrong – and you will get to that – but in the moment of being caught, what do they need? They need connection. They need to know that they are safe and that they are lovable. They need you to still be the person who is able to provide that for them.

One of the mantras that many foster and adoptive parents follow is 'connection before correction'. I love that but for me it misses the first element. It misses you. It makes the focus entirely on the child and I think I've written enough about how unhelpful that is!

My mantra would be ***calm, connect, correct.***

22. The Response Method and Safety Beliefs

It is likely that the response to their behaviour from others in the past has at best not recognised how unsafe you child has been feeling and at worse, led them to feel even more unsafe. You can be different. You can meet their safety behaviours in ways that increase safety for them. Here's some thoughts on how.

You First.

When we respond to our children from a position of being in control of ourselves we automatically increase their safety. All of us are capable of behaving unsafely towards them. We might not like to admit it but under the right (or should I say wrong?) circumstances we are all capable of doing our children harm. Acknowledging that fact makes us much less likely to do the unthinkable.

Keep Yourself in Mind.

Just because you start responding to your child from a position of calm, does not mean you are going to stay feeling that way. As parents we can get good at continually assessing our children but we must also do this for ourselves. Discussions about behaviour do not have to be lengthy. They do not have to happen immediately. They do not have to happen all in one go (although your child does need them resolved in a timeframe they can manage). If you need to take a break to breathe again then do so. Your child will not be able to be calm if you are not yourself.

Positive Touch.

What does your child need to feel calm again? For a lot of children physical touch is very calming. It frustrates me when schools, children's homes and other establishments immediately rule this out as an option. Before fostering and adopting, I worked in three children's homes with 'no touch' policies. My trips to my boss's office to report how I'd broken this rule again became something of a joke.

You see I'd noticed a pattern with some of our young people. They would behave in ways that quickly led to physical restraint. As soon as they were in a hold with a staff member they would immediately relax. If the staff member then released the hold, the young person would return to the previous behaviour and end up being held for a second time. I became curious about this and realised that our ridiculous 'no touch' policy was cutting them off from a vital human need: the need for physical connection.

Many people believe that children who have been physically or sexually harmed should not be touched because it will be too difficult for them. I say these are the children who need touch the most. But the touch they receive needs to be in ways that feel safe for them. Usually this means being touched in a way that is in their control. Often before speaking to my children about their behaviour I will say to them “before we start talking, would you like a hug?”. In the right situation, at the right time, with the right awareness, touch may be incredibly powerful in helping your child to calm. You know them best to decide if this is an option.

Calming Activities.

Aside from touch, there are plenty of other ways to help a child to calm. When they were young my children had a calm box in our lounge that was full of helpful calming activities. They would go to it and spend time there often whilst I was calming myself nearby. When they got older we had a small pop up tent that we filled with blankets, pillows, books and colouring items. One of my children got a lot of use out of a hammock in our back garden. He would swing his stress away. Another would rage with a pair of boxing gloves and a punchbag. Our trampoline got some serious bouncing action too. Now that they are older our children tend to use music to lower their arousal levels. What might help your child if they need to calm before they allow you to connect with them?

Watch Your Defences

Our children engage in fight, flight and freeze behaviours. So, do we. It is very easy when you are in the moment to find yourself attacking and defending one another. Situations can easily and rapidly escalate. The pull for us to become like the parent our children expect us to be can be huge. We mustn't forget this. If we can remain true to ourselves and parent with love and safety then everyone wins. If we don't then everyone loses.

Re-Establish Safety.

If your child's behaviour has resulted in them not being safe, or if they have been responding to an unsafe situation, then safety must be established. Often bringing the child in closer to us and increasing their supervision can achieve this. We will however have to continue to use safety language in explaining this to our child.

Discipline.

'Discipline' has become a taboo word in therapeutic parenting. However, when understood properly and used appropriately, I find it to be an effective response technique.

The word 'discipline' comes from the Latin *word* "Discipulus" which means to learn. Therefore, to discipline a child is to teach them. It is not about 'getting them to behave' but about helping them to grow. So, when you think about what your child has done, what would you like them to learn?

Discipline gives a child boundaries around what is acceptable and what is not. It therefore helps our children to feel safer. When children aren't disciplined, when they are given free-reign to act as they please without consequence, it does not actually make them feel safe. As human beings we need boundaries, especially if we are to live alongside one another successfully. Children need to understand that there are right choices and wrong choices and that all choices have natural consequences.

Children also need to develop their own boundaries to prepare them for future relationships. They need to decide what is appropriate and acceptable behaviour from those around them. Children who have had boundaries that are either too soft or too hard grow into adults who have boundaries that are too soft or too hard. This can lead to disastrous relationships and poor life choices

Setting Consequences.

I never set consequences for my children if a significant link to trauma has caused them to freeze, fight or flight. I understand that in those moments my children had no choice but to respond as they did.

However, in other situations, consequences are set. My preferred approach is to first let my children say what they think would be a suitable consequence. Typically, they are much harsher on themselves then I would ever be! When I caught my son sneaking out of the house late at night the consequence he set himself was to never leave the house again accept for school. Clearly, I was not going to agree to that. The consequence I set was to put a restrictor on his bedroom window so he could not make himself unsafe by climbing on to the roof. I suggested a slightly earlier bedtime for a week to allow him to catch up on all the sleep he had been missing by his late-night activities. I also said I wanted to keep him closer to us until we felt he could make better safety choices. He agreed to it all.

For me the consequences should be a natural response to whatever the child has done. There should be a clear link to teaching them to act differently next time. They should be in proportion to the misdemeanour and should not negatively affect the relationship. After my sons have agreed to consequences I always ask them if they think I have been fair. On the occasions that they say "no" we take time to think and talk about this. Sometimes they are right. I have set consequence based on my feelings rather than what is right for them. On those occasions I apologise, I own my feelings and we renegotiate what those consequences will be.

23. The Response Method and Love Beliefs

When behaviour is the most difficult, we have the greatest opportunity to show love. I'm not in any way saying that is easy. In fact, it is because it is not easy that it has the power to be so transformative. When children behave in unloving ways, they expect an unloving response. It's probably what they have had in the past. When we do the opposite, it sets us apart from their previous relationships and challenges the beliefs that they hold.

You First.

Are you fed up with me beginning with you again? At the start of this book you might have felt pleased to read something that acknowledged your thoughts, feelings, experiences and behaviours. Now you might be sick of me banging on about it!

In difficult situations, my wife and I will often say to one another "step away". What we mean by that is 'step away from the drama'. It's a reminder to not get pulled into the chaos but to remain true to who we are. It's so helpful to have someone remind me of this at times.

In the moment in which I pause before responding to my child I often give myself a little pep talk. I remind myself that I can be in control of who I am and how I act. I tell myself I am a good-enough person and a good-enough parent for them. These days I also remind myself that what has happened is nothing I haven't dealt with before, and often I have dealt with far worse.

In doing so, I increase my sense of self-worth.

Don't De-Skill Yourself

Whatever the situation, your child will likely question whether you can handle it. Let's not buy in to our children's anxieties. Let's not become their relationship template. You have tremendous qualities and skills that make you an excellent parent. How do I know this? You're still reading. This book has become a much longer book than I intended it to be (sorry about that!) but you are still engaging with it.

A social worker assessed you to be good-enough to become a foster or adoptive parent. A panel of experts agreed. More social workers assessed you as a good match for this child. You are trying to learn and grow. You are enough. Don't lose sight of that.

I hope in writing that I have increased your sense of self-worth.

Watch Your Language!

I'm not talking about swearing. Although depending on the age of your child and your own value system that might be something to consider. I'm talking about the language of shame.

When talking to a child about something they did wrong we can all to easily speak in a way that suggests that something about them is wrong. Let's be honest, it's very easy for us to think negatively about them anyway. When my child repeatedly tells me lies I find it difficult not to think of them as a liar. What we do can so easily be seen as a part of who we are. And yet, cognitively at least, I know my son is not a liar. He is someone who is prone to lying when he feels high levels of shame.

Now I'd be lying to you if I told you I had never called him a liar to his face. I have. Again, not something I am proud of. Not only is this wrong, it is also counter-productive. If a child comes to accept being a liar as part of their identity then how are they going to behave? They will lie more and they will feel that they have no control over it because it is, after all, just who they are. All we have done is increase the behaviour we wish to stop.

Avoid the Lecture.

I once heard a well-regarded therapist talk about what he called the 1-minute rule. Parents were permitted to lecture and rant for one minute in order to get it off their chest. He maintained that few parents were able to keep going this long. He hadn't met me.

Lectures are an art form well established in my family. My Nana was particularly good at them. She believed that once a child was old enough to speak and understand then they were old enough to reason with. It was important to her that we understood the error of our ways and learned how to do different next time. And she didn't mind how long she would have to spend teaching us.

My brother and I used to joke about 'Nana Lectures' and roll our eyes if we knew one was coming our way. We'd also get quite annoyed because the natural consequence of her devotion to teaching us was that we were going to miss a lot of our playtime. She had a particular knack for entering into lecture mode just as a favourite tv show was about to come on. As a child I felt this was a frustrating coincidence. As a parent I think she was a genius!

My long discussions with her might have lost me some tv time but they gained me so much more. I knew they were love based. Yes, I knew that they were also a consequence of my actions but they were preferable to other consequences I might have been given. They taught me a lot. Much of my belief system I attribute to the lessons she taught me and I valued the time she spent helping me.

Lectures are not helpful to my children though.

My children do not see them as love based. They can't tolerate such in depth conversations about the behaviours that they believe make them bad people. When they're in shame their thinking brain isn't working and so they aren't able to take on the messages I would want them to hear. Any conversation that goes on for too long will end with them zoning out and me getting frustrated by that.

All lecturing does is allow me to offload my feelings. But expecting my children to manage that when they can't often manage how they feel is unfair and unrealistic.

The method I prefer is to keep conversations really short at the time. Sometimes that is all that is needed. Other times issues can be readdressed at a later point when I'm in better control of myself and they are less ashamed and therefore more open to learning.

Repair Comes from You.

This is hard thing for a lot of parents to understand. It's taken me a while to get my head around it. But the responsibility for repairing the relationship between you and your child is yours. At least initially.

It's hard because it goes completely against our understanding of taking responsibility for our actions, apologising and making it right. If the child has caused the damage then, surely they should initiate the repair, right? It seems unfair for me to suggest otherwise.

It seems unfair because it is unfair. But sadly, there isn't a lot of fairness and justice in the world of fostering and adoption. Yes, your child did the wrong thing but it likely will fall to you to make it right.

The 3B's model advocates that foster and adoptive parents use many of the same parenting techniques that good-enough birth parents do when managing their child's behaviours. If a three-year-old does something naughty then the parent might tell them off. When the child becomes upset by this the parent does not wait for the child to make repair. They will scoop the child up in their arms and initiate the repair themselves.

I'm asking you to do the same for the little three-year-old living inside your child. This will confirm to your child that you do want a relationship with them. It will also challenge any beliefs they might have about relationships being irreparable. Let's not forget that many of our children have seen their poor behaviour lead to placement (and therefore relationship) breakdowns.

So, we model relationship repair by initiating it until a child feels lovable enough to be able to own their mistakes and seek repair themselves.

Repair Consequences

When a child has acted in an unloving way then consequences should be focused on repairing the hurt and healing the relationship. Again, we don't consequence where a child has been trauma triggered into attack, avoid or appease.

However, if, for example, they have just drawn all over a freshly painted wall (it'll be a penis, it's nearly always a penis) then it is entirely suitable to ask them to pay for the paint needed to paint over it. But, it is much more helpful to ask them to either give up their time to repaint the wall with you or to do something nice for the person who's going to be left to do that job.

If one of my children upsets another one then they will often do one of their chores to make amends. The more cognitively capable child has given up his time to help his brother learn to read after calling him 'an idiot'. One of my boys used his pocket money to buy his brother some chocolate after stealing his. And I've a pile of 'sorry' cards that is probably as tall as they are.

Whilst we are on this topic, when I need to apologise to my boys I always offer to do a repair consequence. They always say "no" but I always do one anyway. I've written 'sorry' cards, I've done their chores and I've given up my time for something that they have wanted me to do.

Do Their Consequence Yourself.

Before you think I've lost the plot, let me tell you that this technique is incredibly powerful. Children do generally have a sense of fairness. They know that if they have committed the crime then they should do the time, so to speak. Sometimes, I set a consequence but then do it myself. The boys hate it. They usually go from whinging about the consequence to getting stuck in and doing it with me. They always tell me to stop. The message I send to them is that this consequence needs doing but I love them so much I am going to take it on myself. Sometimes this also comes with me accepting responsibility for placing them in a situation that they struggled to handle.

This is particularly effective with children who engage in consequences as a form of self-punishment. If you have a child that appears to be seeking for you to consequence them then it's worth being curious about what is behind this behaviour. And then change tactic.

I particularly enjoyed the time that I took on their consequence of an earlier bedtime because of late night antics – although my wife was less pleased about that one!

Part 8

Conclusion

24. The 3B's Approach: Next Steps

In the first part of this book I explained my 3B's model to you. We then looked at how it can help us to understand ourselves and our children. In the last section we put this together to consider how we use the Relationship and Response Methods to connect with our children in ways that feel safe and loving.

I truly hope that what I have written has been of value to you. I hope it has offered you genuine empathy for how difficult your role is. I hope it has given you supportive ways to get to know your child and care for him or her in ways that are effective.

We are nearly at the end now. But before I leave you I want to offer you a few thoughts and ideas for implementing this model.

Set Your Own Pace.

This book is the result of ten years of my parenting experience. Switching from traditional parenting to 3B's parenting did not happen overnight. You do not have to rush to implement all your learning. It is much better to make changes slowly and sustain those changes than rush in, get overwhelmed and give up at the first hurdle.

Understand That You Will Be Tested More.

If you change your parenting strategy you will likely find that your child's behaviour initially gets worse rather than better. Put simply, they will need to test out your ability to stick to these new ways of being with them. Although this is really difficult and can appear as though it's not working, it's actually really positive. Children who've been hurt before have to test you before they can feel safe and loved enough to be in relationship with you. Testing is a sign that it is working, so keep going.

Train Your Team.

You can't do this alone. None of us could. One parent is never enough for a poorly attached child, neither is two. You need a team around you of helpful friends, family and professionals. That team needs to be working consistently with the approach you are taking. If you think they will read this book, then great, pass it on. If it helps, then on our families fostering and adoption blog (www.belong-blog.com) subscribers get a free 5-day email course that outlines the basics of the 3B's model. I also write weekly blog posts on a variety of parenting concerns.

Continue Your Personal Development

I hope that I have managed to write this book in a way that balances your needs with the needs of your child. Personal development has been such a strong feature of my fostering and adoption story. I would encourage you to continue thinking about yourself and your needs. For me personally that meant therapy, developing relationships in which I could be vulnerable and lots of reading and training. Your personal development may require something else. Whatever you do, I do believe that the parents who survive fostering and adoption do so because they are able to become self-aware as well as child-aware.

Continue to Learn.

You can go to seminars, training and read about other ideas and incorporate them into the 3B's model. Like I said at the start, I wasn't looking to develop something completely different. I wanted to develop a parenting approach that integrates some of the great ideas already out there and allows me to add my own ideas from experience.

A parent said to me recently "I don't use Dan Hughe's PLACE model anymore, now I use Non-Violent Resistance" and I thought 'Why does it have to be either or?'.

We don't need to stick religiously to one idea. One model is not likely to meet the very many challenges our children bring to us. Jumping between different parenting models does not help us to be the consistent parents our children need us to be. But if we use the 3B's basic principle as our way of integrating our understanding and practice, then we can use lots of different ideas and bring them together as a whole.

Your child may be very violent. An NVR technique may be really helpful to increase the safety and reduce that behaviour. Following this with a PLACE approach to conversation might address the shame issues. You might use the principles of Restorative Parenting when setting repair consequences or some of the great games of Theraplay to develop your relationship with them and so on.

Don't worry if you have no idea about these different parenting and therapy models. All therapeutic models work on the same basis that you have already learned: they all seek to develop a relationship, reduce shame and increase safety. For now, you don't need to do any more reading but they are all worth exploring later, when you feel ready.

As long as it upholds the relationship and is safe and loving then please do use it. You know your child best, not me. So, feel empowered to make the right choices for you both.

Ask for Help

Your assessment to become a parent was all focused on ensuring you had the qualities and skills to meet your child's needs. The fantasy is that we all ride off into the sunset and live happily ever after. But the reality is likely to be very different.

It's ok to ask for help. In fact, I would say that it's essential. My wife and I came into parenting with over 30 years' experience of working with looked after children. That's a lot more than most foster and adoptive parents have. We've struggled. We've needed help. We are now post-graduate trained, one of us as a psychotherapist and the other as a therapeutic youth-worker. We still struggle at times. We still need help.

Asking for the help you need is not failing. Failing to ask for the help you need is.

Let Me Help You If I Can.

My passion is for supporting foster and adoptive parents. I think that there are a lot of professionals available to work with your children but often the thoughts, feelings and desires of the parent go unnoticed. I also believe that as parents we lack safe spaces in which to explore what the demands of our role mean for us. I want to support you in any way I can.

For those of you living in the UK I offer training, counselling and psychotherapy through my business Belong Therapeutic Support (www.belongts.com). On a worldwide scale I offer training and parenting ideas on our family blog (www.belong-blog.com). On that website you will also find a list of books I recommend for when you are ready to read some more.

I hope to keep writing books and articles whilst there are people still willing to read them. Please do provide me feedback so I know what is helpful and what is not. If there is ever anything you would like me to write about please contact me via belong@belongts.com

I wish you and your children all the best for the future and hope to meet you some day.

Love Fi

Epilogue.

It was February 2009 that I sat on those stairs and cried. So much has happened in the nine years since.

The two children who lived with me then were joined in the July by their younger brother. In five months I had gone from feeling completely overwhelmed by two children, to feeling like I could manage another. It wasn't easy by any stretch of the imagination, but it was easier.

I love my children. I love that the brothers who were destined to be growing up apart from one another in foster care have had the opportunity to grow up together instead. I love seeing them grow both as individuals and also in their relationships with us. I love that I, my wife and our relationship have survived it all.

When I started writing this book it was late 2015. We had just adopted our children and offered them the legal permanence that they craved and needed. We were in a good place and set to continue that way. Then life happened. Over a two-year period, we experienced the deaths of six family members and close friends. Six people who we were all close to, four of whom were key members of our support network.

I've written about cumulative loss before but never personally experienced its devasting effects like so many fostered and adopted children have – not having the chance to recover from losing one person before losing another. I found it incredibly difficult, we all did.

One of our children found it particularly hard. He began behaving in ways that were incredibly unsafe for him and for the rest of our family. He became convinced that he was going to lose us. He saw this as inevitable and began to push for it to happen. He hit his self-destruct button and the rest of us became collateral damage.

In the midst of our own grief we reached out for professionals and services to help us. Sadly, they didn't. We encountered so many people who could have been great assets to our family if they had the knowledge and experience of trauma required. Instead they became a hinderance. They saw him as a teenager seeking power and control through defiance and aggression. He wasn't. He was a young boy struggling to deal with a very difficult situation and fearing he was going to lose everyone who meant anything to him.

In the end, his behaviour became too unsafe for him to live in a family home. He was moved into residential care. I cannot begin to tell you the level of devastation that I felt. It was like a part of me had been ripped away. I feared that I had lost him for good, that he would see it as a massive rejection and never speak to me again.

For several months this played out. He refused to see us or was unkind when he did. We tried to support the team of professionals now around him but found them to be unwilling to work with us. We were seen as the parents who had failed. Of course, the reality was the opposite. All of this had happened because our son had formed an attachment to us and was terrified of losing it. But it wasn't seen that way. We were called names, judged as both too lenient and too strict and controlling and removed from the decisions around his care.

Without our involvement things went from bad to worse and we watched as our son became more unsafe and more traumatised in the process. I stopped writing. My self-worth took a big hit and all of the trauma of those months caught up with me. I questioned what right I had to support foster and adoptive parents when my son was in 'adoption breakdown'. I will always hate that term.

Then I realised what I hope I have already conveyed to you. We can't fix our children. We aren't responsible for what has led them to develop in the ways they have and we can't control what may happen to them in the future. All I can ever do is offer him a relationship that is safe and loving. What he does with that offer is up to him.

And so, I (we) did that. We continued to be available to him. We continued to be clear that we loved him. On the occasions that his behaviour towards us was unsafe we remained consistent in saying that we loved him, just not what he was doing. For the months that he wouldn't communicate with us at all we sent cards, we sent gifts, we left voicemails and messages. It was heart breaking but we held on the fact that for us the relationship is everything.

Then one day he called. He called, he apologised and he asked to see us again. The next day we met up. We cried together. We laughed together. We held each other. We talked. We talked a lot. And slowly we began to repair the relationship.

That was only three months ago. I don't know if he will ever live with us again (he's approaching adulthood). What I do know is that our relationship can withstand anything.

And what he and his brothers know for sure is that they belong with us.

Acknowledgements.

This book has been a long time in the making. It encompasses both my professional and personal journeys alongside fostered and adopted young people and parents. For that reason, I have many people to thank for their time, wisdom and generosity. In alphabetical order, here are just some of them.

Caroline Weeks – When training as a therapist I never expected to meet such a great friend for life. You inspire me in so many ways and have truly been there for me through the good times and the bad. Thank you is not enough.

Celia Dawson – My spelling and grammar expert! Thank you so much for reading the draft of this book, correcting all my mistakes and showing me where I need to be a better communicator. These are the only pages you haven't checked so I hope I spell everything crorectly here!

Dzmitry Karpuk – It's always helpful to have a systemic family therapist on hand when you are trying to put the model in your head on to paper in a way that other people will hopefully understand! You challenge me to learn more and to be a better therapist and person. Thank you.

Jane Foulkes – You were the therapist I phoned after crying on the stairs that night. That fact that you are still working alongside our family nearly 10 years later is something I am truly thankful for. Your insight, patience and commitment to me and my family has led us to where we are today. Thank you.

Jonathan Mason – For an adopter to have a therapist who just 'gets it' is a special thing. Thank you for being their when I needed to vent, for never shaming me in those moments when I felt like burying them under the patio and for helping Gail and I to 'trauma-proof' our relationship. We are both incredibly grateful

Kate Tait – Where would I be without one my closest friends? You knew nothing about the world of fostering and adoption but have willingly been at my side every step of the way. Always on hand with a glass of wine and a shoulder to cry on. Amazing really given that the first time you met my son he knocked your sons tooth out! Thank you is not enough.

Matt Davies – It is so rare for a social worker to bring a child into care, support them through fostering and remain in touch with them after they are adopted. Thank you for allowing us in those early days to experiment with a new parenting approach which other professionals around us could not understand.

Mica Douglas – I am so fortunate to have you in my life. Your support on both a professional and a personal level has meant the world to me. I look forward to continuing to work together.

Special thanks also go to my family who have been so incredibly supportive. You have accepted my children in the same way you would accept any children and for that I am very grateful. I also appreciate the way you will continue to support us with babysitting and respite in the future :-)

I also want to recognise the many amazing foster and adoptive parents who we have met over the years. Your willingness to support us and laugh and cry alongside us has been a tremendous blessing. Thank you.

To the great writers and trainers I have had to learn from. Your knowledge, wisdom and understanding made what felt impossible become achievable. I would particularly mention **Mica Douglas, Cas Heath-Faye, Kim Golding, Louise Bomber, Daniel Siegel, Daniel Hughes, Jazz Kang, Basia Spalek, Celia Dawson, Dzmitry Karpuk, Babette Rothschild and Bruce Perry.** Some of you prove that great learning can come from reading books – I hope that this book offers to others something of what you all have given to me.

Finally, my biggest thanks go to four very special people.

Gail, parenting has been my biggest challenge and I would not have wanted to do it with anyone other than you. You have been there to step in on the many occasions I have felt overwhelmed. You have listened patiently to my rants about children's services. You have supported me through the triggering of my own trauma. You have shown me what true safety and love feels like. Most importantly, in the seventeen years we have been together you have never stopped bringing me a cup of tea every morning. That's love.

And finally, to my children, **Hayden, Shane and Scott**. Without you this book would not have been possible. Literally. You amaze me every day. Your willingness to take a risk on family life is incredible. I could not be happier that each of you came into my life. You have taught me so much about myself and, although it has been very difficult at times, I would not wish to parent anyone else. You have made my life complete. I am excited to meet the young men that I know you are capable of being.

Always remember, I cannot love you more and I will not love you less. No matter what.